Percy Bysshe Shelley

Andrew Keanie

GREENWICH EXCHANGE
LONDON

Greenwich Exchange, London

Percy Bysshe Shelley
©Andrew Keanie 2011

First published in Great Britain in 2011
All rights reserved

Printed and bound by **imprint**digital.net
Typesetting and layout by Jude Keen, London
Tel: 020 8355 4541
Cover design by December Publications, Belfast
Tel: 028 90286559
Cover image: Percy Bysshe Shelley
©Mary Evans Picture Library

Greenwich Exchange Website: www.greenex.co.uk

Cataloguing in Publication Data is available from the
British Library.

ISBN: 978-1-906075-59-0

Could the reader, who has perhaps seen him held up in the pages of the *Quarterly Review* as a demon, have transported himself to the beautiful Bay of Lerici in the Gulf of Spezia, and beheld a fragile youth moving about upon the earth like a gentle spirit, imagining incessant plans for promoting the welfare of the great circle of mankind, while he formed the happiness of the little one in which he moved, and recreating himself with music, literature, and poetic reveries while he floated … upon the blue waves of the Mediterranean – how little would he dream that he was gazing upon the traduced and calumniated Percy Bysshe Shelley! (*The Paris Monthly Review*)

> And that I walked thus proudly crowned withal
> Is that 'tis my distinction; if I fall,
> I shall not weep out of the vital day,
> To-morrow dust, nor wear a dull decay. ('Crowned', 1821)

To Emma

Contents

1

A Spirit in a Material World

In 1811, Percy Bysshe Shelley (1792-1822), a first-year undergraduate at University College, Oxford, and his friend Thomas Jefferson Hogg (1792-1862), jointly produced the anonymous pamphlet, 'The Necessity of Atheism'. As the title suggests, the publication was deliberately controversial, though the argument is also classical:

> it is urged that man knows that whatever is, must either have had a beginning or existed from all eternity, he also knows that whatever is not eternal must have had a cause. – Where this is applied to the existence of the universe, it is necessary to prove that it was created, until that is clearly demonstrated, we may reasonably suppose that it has endured from all eternity. ('The Necessity of Atheism')

However, in addition to the liberal Enlightenment warmth inspiriting the prose, there is also a little of the teenage rebel's delight in tapping publicly at the fault lines of platitudinous piety: "In a case where two propositions are diametrically opposite, the mind believes that which is less incomprehensible; it is easier to suppose that the Universe has existed from all eternity, than to conceive a being capable of creating it" ('The Necessity of Atheism'). The eighteen-year-old pamphleteer was already known as the author of two Gothic novels: *Zastrozzi* (1810) and *St Irvyne or the Rosicrucian* (1810). The following passage from chapter 15 of *Zastrozzi* reveals Shelley's debt to Matthew 'Monk' Lewis' (1775-1818) *The Monk* (1796), including something of a fascination for how violence and sexual passion can overlap each other:

> "Die, detested wretch," exclaimed Mathilda, in a paroxysm of rage, as she violently attempted to bathe the stiletto in the life-blood of her rival; but Julia starting aside, the weapon slightly wounded her neck, and the ensanguined stream stained her alabaster bosom. She fell on the floor, but suddenly starting up, attempted to escape her bloodthirsty persecutor. Nerved anew by this futile attempt to escape her vengeance,

the ferocious Mathilda seized Julia's floating hair, and holding her back with fiend-like strength, stabbed her in a thousand places; and, with exulting pleasure, again and again buried the dagger up to the hilt in her body, even after all the remains of life were annihilated. At last the passions of Mathilda, exhausted by their own violence, sank into deadly calm; she threw the dagger violently from her, and contemplated the terrific scene before her with a sullen gaze.

The young writer was in the process of expressing his own forbidden desires, and he would be preserving only their quintessence by his late twenties. The sense of post-coital enervation suggested by Mathilda's "sullen gaze" would reappear, in 1820, as the "sad satiety" all too familiar to human beings, but unknown to the skylark soaring unencumbered by human destructiveness.

The following passage from chapter 10 of *St Irvyne* looks autobiographical (though it is ostensibly Ginotti narrating his story to Wolfstein):

From my earliest youth, before it was quenched by complete satiation, *curiosity*, and a desire of unveiling the latent mysteries of nature, was the passion by which all the other emotions of my mind were intellectually organized. This desire first led me to cultivate, and with success, the various branches of learning which led to the gates of wisdom. I then applied myself to the cultivation of philosophy, and the éclat with which I pursued it, exceeded my most sanguine expectations. – Natural philosophy ... became the peculiar science to which I directed my eager enquiries; thence was I led into a train of labyrinthine meditations.

The speaker of Shelley's later poem, *Alastor or the Spirit of Solitude* (1815), would suggest what one of these "eager enquiries" was: "I have made my bed / In charnels and on coffins" (23-4). One does not have to take this literally to recognise a mind acquainted with uncomfortable darkness and depth.

Even of his passionate admirers, many have not got beyond the dramatic impression of the poet, attractive and strange, with the beating waves or gusting winds uplifting his hair; or as Hogg once put it, "like a spirit that had just descended from the sky; like a demon risen at that moment out of the ground" (Peck, I, 278); or as Leigh Hunt (1784-1859) once put it, "like a spirit that had darted out of its orb and found itself another planet" (*Lord Byron and his Contemporaries*, 1828). But how many have felt the power and sincerity of his poetry? How many have profoundly felt its vital influence? Shelley, known as 'the Eton Atheist' and 'Mad Shelley' (Holmes, 19), was not really known.

He had much to say about what was wrong with society, "our state, / This dim vast vale of tears, vacant and desolate" ('Hymn to Intellectual Beauty' II), and he would have much more to say about how "Poets ... the unacknowledged legislators of the world", could put things right, if given the chance: "never joy illumed my brow / Unlinked with hope" ('Hymn to Intellectual Beauty' VI). "God help us!" exclaimed the former radical writer, Robert Southey (1774-1843), in January 1812, "the world wants mending, though he [Shelley] did not set about it exactly in the right way" (Peck, I, 204), which seems as much to illuminate Southey's character as Shelley's. If the "right way" meant a reverent submission to authority, then Shelley undoubtedly did "set about it" in the 'wrong' way.

The following, from an obituary on Shelley, is an example of the kind of reportage that habituates an appreciable percentage of the (voting) public to palliative cynicism, influencing them not to read or think beyond their weekly papers. On 5 August 1822, the London *Courier* pronounced that "Shelley, the writer of some infidel poetry, has been drowned; *now* he knows whether there is a God or no." So much for the thinking electorate wished for so passionately by the poet. And so much for that electorate's access to exalted vision. Journalists and academics then, as now, had prejudices to pander to and thence money to collect.

Shelley's "passion for reforming the world", as he called it in the Preface to *Prometheus Unbound* (1819), was routinely loathed and rejected by that world: "But thus much I do not seek to conceal from myself, that I am an outcast from human society; my name is execrated by all who understand its entire import – by those very beings whose happiness I ardently desire." (*Letters*, I, 517) Yet he did not give up. He would never have heeded Arthur Schopenhauer (1788-1860): "The man who comes into the world with the notion that he is really going to instruct it in matters of the highest importance, may thank his stars if he escapes with a whole skin" (*Counsels and Maxims*, 78). Sir Walter Scott (1771-1832) gave Shelley some sound advice (unheeded) in May 1811:

> I would ... caution you against an enthusiasm which while it argues an excellent disposition and a feeling heart, requires to be watched and restrained, tho' not repressed. It is apt, if too much indulged, to engender a fastidious contempt for the ordinary business of the world, and gradually unfit us for the exercise of the useful and domestic virtues, which depend greatly on our not exalting our feelings above the temper of well-ordered society. (Peck, I, 38)

These are essentially conservative concepts. Scott saw Shelley's brilliance of mind and his impatience with the conventional arrangements of life. Scott did not positively appreciate the inextricable and explosive nature of the two characteristics. And he does not seem to have been aware of the possibility of the inferiority of his way of living to Shelley's: he was implying (above) a rebuke of Shelley for emotionalism, but what he was really objecting to was Shelley's unguarded expression of emotion. Perhaps it is these unguarded expressions that the reader of Shelley should be most grateful for.

Shelley was clear about what he was *not* doing as a writer. He did not offer "a reasoned system", and he did not want "the direct enforcement of reform". He had in mind something that men of the (commonsense) world tend not to take seriously: "beautiful idealisms of moral excellence" (Preface, *Prometheus Unbound*). He formulated an "aware[ness] that until the mind can love, and admire, and trust, and hope, and endure, reasoned principles of moral conduct are seeds cast upon the highway of life which the unconscious passenger tramples into dust" (Preface, *Prometheus Unbound*). This is an instance of Shelley's metaphysical precision of thought that impresses few people because they cannot have it reified; it would involve, somehow, the replacement in people of negative with positive habits of thinking. One might see psychological acuity in the aspiration, and argue that it foreshadows the practice of 'cognitive therapy' with which the droves of twentieth- and twenty-first-century psychotherapists, social workers and their administrators have undertaken to commodify the 'known' (and ignore the unknown) aspects of the troubled western mind.

Shelley's vision is more radiant and essential than the cleverness and power of memory so busily exhibited by uninspired people. It represents what *is*, and is always present, including feeling and emotion. The poet includes the whole cosmos, the phenomenal as well as the noumenal. He declares the presence of the unknown:

> Let every seed that falls
> In silent eloquence unfold its store
> Of argument; infinity within,
> Infinity without, belie creation;
> The exterminable spirit it contains
> Is Nature's only God ... (*Queen Mab*, 19-24).

The unknown is anathema to most people, especially educated or professional people, who can become indignant at the mildest inference that the exertions that got them where they are today were not necessarily best applied:

> ... but human pride
> Is skilful to invent most serious names
> To hide its ignorance. (*Queen Mab*, 24-6)

The majority of readers want to be indulged in their own comfort zones, and poets in the twentieth century from John Betjeman (1906-84) at his worst to John Burnside (1955-) have provided them with the requisite literature. Many readers tend to feel chagrined by the presence of unfamiliar colours and urgent voices. Shelley saw such easily piqued complacency as a sort of Bastille to be stormed by the radical energies of real life and truth. William Rossetti (1829-1919) would say that "As an iconoclast and an idealist" Shelley "took the only position in which he could advantageously work as a reformer. To outrage his contemporaries".

Look at the apparently serene and predictable statement of public grief in the following passage from Shelley's *Address to the People on the Death of the Princess Charlotte* (1817). The first ten sentences appear to deliver a ready rush of journalistic sympathy for the recently deceased Princess Charlotte:

> Mourn then, People of England. Clothe yourselves in solemn black. Let the bells be tolled. Think of mortality and change. Shroud yourselves in solitude and the gloom of sacred sorrow. Spare no symbol of universal grief. Weep – mourn – lament. Fill the great City – fill the boundless fields with lamentation and the echo of groans. A beautiful Princess is dead: she who should have been the Queen of her beloved nation and whose posterity should have ruled it forever ... She was amiable and would have become wise, but she was young, and in the flower of youth the despoiler came. LIBERTY is dead.

The last short sentence is a shock to the cant-consuming system. There is something in it of the guerrilla ambush, the news of which is bound to elicit strong feelings. The writer is facing unpleasant facts, and creating a republic of words in which he can exist more powerfully than he does elsewhere. Princess Charlotte's death happened to coincide with the public hanging and quartering of three Pentridge Revolution leaders. Seizing the royalist mood of the moment – but by no means forgetting the government skulduggery leading to the deaths of Jeremiah Brandreth, Isaac Ludlam and William Turner (Holmes, 384-6) – Shelley makes startlingly valid the moral superiority of his metaphorical bereavement to the tears more popularly shed for Princess Charlotte. Having sprung his trap – "LIBERTY is dead" – in the centre of the nation's sorrow, he pursues the logic of his metaphor to its extravagantly revolutionary conclusion:

> If One has died who was like her that should have ruled over this land, like Liberty, young, innocent, and lovely, know that the power through which that one perished was God, and that it was a private grief. But *man* has murdered Liberty ... Let us follow the corpse of British Liberty slowly and reverentially to its tomb; and if some glorious Phantom should appear and make its throne of broken swords and sceptres and royal crowns trampled in the dust, let us say that the Spirit of Liberty has arisen from its grave and left all that was gross and mortal there, and kneel down and worship it as our Queen. (Holmes, 388)

There was, however, a problem. Shelley's publisher, Charles Ollier, was scared of getting into trouble with the authorities and therefore printed only a limited edition of the pamphlet. Shelley did not have the contemporary political impact on a large reading public that he should have had. This would not be the last missed opportunity.

Would readers have been prepared to believe in the superiority of Shelley's poetic alternative over the more prevalent, royalist sentiment in circulation at the time? Probably not. Writers who would make friends and influence people tend not to express themselves in such incorrigible terms. Hence the suburban gardens "gift-wrapped in dew", as described by the prize-winning, Arts Council grant recipient, John Burnside. And hence the fact that generations of British schoolchildren have learned to recite Wordsworth's 'Daffodils', but remained unaware of the tortured political uncertainties with which Wordsworth produced the 'Residence in France' section of *The Prelude* like a painful pearl.

Shelley's insights are often elemental, and they imply that if Revolution comes not as naturally as the leaves to a tree it better not come at all. But many of these insights have lain in dust and handwriting for over a hundred years:

> the spring rebels not against
> winter but it succeeds it –
> the dawn rebels not
> against night but it
> disperses it – (Wroe, 265)

Publishers often found Shelley's writing too dangerously subversive, or too obscure. In terms of publications, sales, and acclaim, Shelley was not particularly successful in his day. Even in a comparatively encouraging contemporary review of work that Shelley *did* get published, the poet's lack of chemistry with his nation's readers does not go unmentioned:

Mr Shelley can never become a popular poet. He does not sufficiently link himself with man; he is too visionary for the intellect of the generality of his readers, and is ever immersed in the clouds of religions and meta-physical speculations. His opinions are but skeletons, and he does not sufficiently embody them to render them intelligible. ('On the Philosophy and Poetry of Shelley', Gold's *London Magazine*, 1821)

By the time he wrote his 10,000-word essay, *A Defence of Poetry* (1821), he had formulated and refined what he was about as a poet (though the world would, of course, continue to be just as foolish and wicked as it had been on the poet's arrival into it):

All the authors of revolutions in opinion are not only necessarily poets as they are inventors, nor even as their words unveil the permanent analogy of things by images which participate in the light of truth; but as their periods are harmonious and rhythmical, and contain in themselves the elements of verse; being the echo of the eternal music.

The idea of the poet as an inventor is of its time. Just as the Cornish chemist Humphry Davy (1778-1829) invented the safety lamp to enable miners to see underground more safely than before, so Shelley's poetic inventions could "purge … from our inward sight the film of familiarity which obscures from us the wonder of our deep being." The Latin word for invention, *inventus*, means discovery, which is particularly appropriate to Shelley's visionary poetry: the poet discovered, or rediscovered, "the hidden beauty of the world" (*A Defence of Poetry*), or, as he had his chorus of spirits define their provenance in Act IV of *Prometheus Unbound*,

the mind
Of humankind,
Which was late so dusk, and obscure, and blind …

that deep abyss
Of wonder and bliss,
Whose caverns are crystal palaces (93-101).

Most people automatically ignore the presence of essential reality when it is intangible. And people tend to shy away from sharing spiritual recognitions that call forth the sort of words (such as 'holy' or 'soul') that the march of Enlightenment thinking and the subsequent race of rampant materialism has rendered almost ridiculous looking. Shelley's use of the word "spirits" – like his use of the word "atheist" – is part of the rough magic of his alienated mode of eloquence. "The Atheist," he wrote in *A Refutation of Deism* (1814),

> is a monster among men ... He dreads no judge but his own conscience, he fears no hell but the loss of his self-esteem. He is not to be restrained by punishments, for death is divested of its terror, and whatever enters into his heart to conceive, that he will not scruple to execute ...

Shelley's insights are not just into himself and his own alienated psychology. He does not merely assume that something has universal significance just because it has happened to him. He is endowed with access to the universal – the sufferings and aspirations of humanity's collective mind and secret thoughts. He is driven from within to beat fiercely upon the prison-door of the reality in which most other people would settle. And if thinking divine thoughts is going to make one dissatisfied with mortality, then it is quite naturally also going to make one unhappy with anyone imposing restrictions of any kind:

> As divinest Shakespeare's might
> Fills Avon and the world with light
> Like omniscient power which he
> Imaged 'mid mortality ...
> A quenchless lamp, by which the heart,
> Sees things unearthly ... ('Lines Written Among the Euganean Hills', 196-203).

The mysterious contradiction between reality and ideality, one of the most profound questions of ontology, is strongly shown in the above lines. Shelley knows that the poet carries a tremendous burden. He knows that the poet's struggle calls forth practically no recognition from his contemporaries. And yet his will to write persists. It is not for nothing that the "Soul" in Andrew Marvell's (1621-78) poem, 'A Dialogue, between the Resolved Soul and Created Pleasure', asks: "If things of sight such heavens be, / What heavens are those sights we cannot see?"

Many eminent critics, including Matthew Arnold, W.H. Auden and Marilyn Butler, have not found particularly compelling in Shelley (or in anyone) the central issue of "thought-wingèd Liberty" ('Lines Written Among the Euganean Hills', 207). Instead, at their most sympathetic – or rather their least unsympathetic – they have, for example, understood that the poet conceived a fresh means of political struggle. The passive resistance to tyranny in 'The Mask of Anarchy' (1819) showed Mahatma Gandhi (1869-1948) the most effective way for the people of India to emancipate themselves from British colonial rule:

> 'And if then the tyrants dare,
> Let them ride among you there,
> Slash, and stab, and maim, and hew;
> What they like, that let them do.
>
> 'With folded arms and steady eyes,
> And little fear, and less surprise,
> Look upon them as they slay,
> Till their rage has died away.
>
> 'Then they will return with shame
> To the place from which they came;
> And the blood thus shed will speak
> In hot blushes on their cheek. ('The Mask of Anarchy', LXXXV-LXXXVII)

But the King James Bible already contained similar wisdom: "If thine enemy be hungry, give him bread to eat; and if he be thirsty, give him water to drink" (Proverbs: 25: 21). "But I say unto you, Love your enemies, bless them that curse you, do good to them that hate you, and pray for them which despitefully use you, and persecute you" (St. Matthew: 5: 44). "Therefore if thine enemy hunger, feed him; if he thirst, give him drink: for in so doing thou shalt heap coals of fire on his head" (Romans: 12: 20.) In some of the freer modern translations of the Bible, "thou shalt heap coals of fire on his head" becomes "you will make them burn with shame". At any rate, Shelley had an aptitude for sifting ancient texts and revitalising the real meaning of wise spiritual guidance. He detested the practice of organised Christianity.

Some critics have celebrated Shelley's 'street protest' songs as his highest achievements. Others have derided them as the dispensable vapourings of a 'Riviera socialist' who, in his own words, "lay asleep in Italy" ('The Mask of Anarchy', I) at the time of the governmentally masterminded atrocity in Manchester known as the Peterloo Massacre (1819). Implicit in both these views is the assumption that politics and political 'realities' form the sea-level from which all writers, including visionary poets, must take all their bearings.

Leaving politics – "something other than human life", as William Blake said

– aside for the time being, it is worth considering another source of inspiration predominantly significant to Shelley: the poet's sense of wonder, often situated on the border between science and the imagination. One important influence on Shelley, Samuel Taylor Coleridge, intended to "be able to evolve all the five senses, that is, to deduce from them *one sense*, & to state their growth, & the cause of their difference – & in this evolvement to solve the problem of Life and Consciousness." (*Coleridge Letters*, II, 706) Another contemporary poet, John Keats, was aware of the mysteriously interconnected vastnesses of outer and inner space: "Then felt I like some watcher of the skies / When a new planet swims into his ken" ('On First Looking into Chapman's Homer'). Shelley was influenced by the work of the physician, botanist and poet Erasmus Darwin (1731-1802), particularly *The Botanic Garden* (1791), which was the best-selling long poem in English of the 1790s:

> "Let there be Light!", proclaimed the Almighty Lord,
> Astonished Chaos heard the potent word;
> Through all his realms the kindling ether runs
> And the mass starts into a million Suns.
>
> Earths round each Sun with quick explosions burst,
> And second Planets issue from the first;
> Bend as they journey with projectile force,
> In bright eclipses their reluctant course;
> Orbs wheel in orbs, round centres centres roll,
> And form, self-balanced, one revolving whole.

Darwin's copious notes to this poem – on chemistry, cosmology, geology, meteorology and physics – formed a comprehensive account of contemporary science. Shelley was so impressed by Darwin's achievement that he would provide similarly learned and copious notes to his *Queen Mab* (1813).

Visionary poetry is not restricted to the poet's personal concerns, however complex and unstable the construction of his character traits. Shelley himself, however, in 1811, in the vainglory of youth and in the grip of a violent desire to eschew cultural prohibitions, affixed the inflammatory title, 'The Necessity of Atheism', to what was really a rather mild (not to mention prentice) philosophical argument. He had to put it in the windows of the Oxford bookshops himself because no one would publish it. He sent copies to the bishops and the heads of the colleges. As a result of his early drive for recognition and notoriety, Shelley ended up misleading the majority of his contemporaries, and posterity, about what he really was.

2

Perennial Wisdom and Political Exile

With maturity, which developed more rapidly in Shelley than it did in any other poet, he would not write on behalf of any theory, or with deference to any fad or fashion of contemporary thought. He would write from within the tradition of philosophy, or wisdom, known as perennial. The perennial wisdom flows through all ages, often out of sight, and sometimes emerging to revitalise humanity:

> ... one majestic River,
> The breath and blood of distant lands, forever
> Rolls its loud waters to the ocean waves,
> Breathes its swift vapors to the circling air. ('Mont Blanc', IV, 123-6)

It is difficult to convert into discursive language "The everlasting universe of things" ('Mont Blanc', I, 1) without evaporating the invaluable unknown out of it. Its flow through the ages is a special source of inspiration to visionary writers (such as Shakespeare and Marvell), yet it has been overlooked by practically all educators. Coleridge caught it spectacularly in 'Kubla Khan' (1797), a poem which has been taught in schools. But some of us may realise that despite having classroom memories of the works of Coleridge, Shelley, and Wordsworth we have somehow imbibed the additional idea that we can rise to our full stature only at a remove from the poets: we may judge them in terms of their own expansive ideas and values (beauty, love, rebellion, risk), yet we must live in smaller ways (conformity, safety, utility), which represent the criteria above which we might perhaps soar occasionally in thought, and preferably in our 'spare' time. For the visionary poet,

> ... Thought
> Alone, and its quick elements, Will, Passion,
> Reason, Imagination, cannot die;
> They are what that which they regard appears,
> The stuff whence mutability can weave

All that it hath dominion o'er – worlds, worms,
Empires, and superstitions. What has thought
To do with time, or place, or circumstance? (*Hellas*, 795-802)

If we were to really take heed of these words, they could

shake
The earth on which [we] stand ...
They cast on all things, surest, brightest, best, –
Doubt, insecurity, astonishment. (*Hellas*, 787-91)

Most of us have been trained to collude in the construction and maintenance of a comfortable mediocrity that prevents life from inconveniencing us with a superior, and therefore often more joyous (and often more painful), quality of consciousness. This is why, when not 'on the make', we devote so much of ourselves to essentially absurd activities, from weeding the garden to reading the *Guardian*.

The perennial wisdom is almost completely unknown to the modern mind conditioned by modern education. And yet the following view of the fugitive nature of ultimate reality, expressed by Thomas Taylor the Platonist (1758-1835) – the first English translator of the entire works of Plato, and of whose works all the major English Romantic poets were aware – is as applicable in the twenty-first century as it was when first written:

> ... in short, to pursue matter through its infinite divisions, and wander in its dark labyrinths, is the employment of the philosophy in vogue. But surely the energies of intellect are more worthy [of] our concern than the operations of sense ... Where ... is the microscope which can discern what is smallest in nature? Where the telescope that can see at what point in the universe wisdom first began? Since, then, there is no portion of matter which may not be the subject of experiments without end, let us betake ourselves to the regions of mind, where all things are bounded in intellectual measure; where everything is permanent and beautiful, eternal and divine. (from Taylor's Introduction to Plotinus' 'An Essay On the Beautiful')

Shelley could not simply forget about such regions of mind whose universal nature he could intuitively comprehend, the quality of whose being he could sensitively feel, and with whom he could sustain a vital relationship. He would not think the priceless, timeless gift away in exchange for the "philosophy in vogue":

> Thou mayst behold
> How cities, on which empire sleeps enthroned,
> Bow their towered crests to mutability. (*Hellas*, 844-6)

He could not – and would not – bear the omission of the essential. He could hardly bear how other people insisted on the omission:

> Facts are not what we want to know in poetry, in history, in the lives of individual men, in satire, or panegyric. They are the mere divisions, the arbitrary points on which we hang, and to which we refer those delicate and evanescent hues of mind, which language delights and instructs us in precise proportion as it expresses. (*Letters*, II, 277)

For Shelley, the essential remains present regardless of the materialization of air balloons, underground safety lamps or steam engines. For Shelley, the essential

> Floats though unseen among us, visiting
> This various world with its inconstant wing
> As summer winds that creep from flower to flower;
> Like moonbeams that behind some piny mountain shower ... ('Hymn to Intellectual Beauty', I).

The idea of interpreting infinitely multifaceted and multidimensional life with the gimcrack terminology of "this wrong world" ('Letter to Maria Gisborne', 160) is abhorrent to a poet determined to include "th[e] forgotten dream" (*Hellas*, 842) and "the uncreated deep" (*Hellas*, 858) in his contemplations. Shelley pursues the essence of the very mystery that is left out of most other poetry:

> It visits with inconstant glance
> Each human heart and countenance;
> Like hues and harmonies of evening,
> Like clouds in starlight widely spread,
> Like memory of music fled,
> Like aught that for its grace may be
> Dear, and yet dearer for its mystery. ('Hymn to Intellectual Beauty', I)

His emotions, interests and prejudices are present as he selects, relates and sifts. He is working in a field, the human mystery, in which human emotions, interests and prejudices are pervasively relevant; a field moreover in which experiment is impossible. To most people he appears to play a strange, or even ludicrous, game.

All his efforts relate to the single question whose very unanswerable nature (if the poet is not considered beneath contempt for contemplating it) often elicits mirth more than wonder: "What is life?" (Holmes, 297) When the poet is perceived as continuing to amuse himself with the pursuit of something that cannot be pursued, he is unlikely to gain many admirers. He has no words with which to make people believe they will receive from him something he cannot give:

> Thoughts and feelings arise, with or without our will, and we employ words to express them. We are born, and our birth is unremembered, and our infancy remembered but in fragments; we live on, and in living we lose the apprehension of life. How vain it is to think that we can penetrate the mystery of our being! (Holmes, 297-8)

Lord Byron's worldly-wise friends John Cam Hobhouse (1786-1869) and Scrope Davies (1782-1852) were unwilling to acknowledge, or incapable of recognising, the extent of Shelley's influence on Byron's work. When Hobhouse read the first two cantos of Byron's *Childe Harold's Pilgrimage* (1812) he said "there is an air of mystery and metaphysics about it", but he denied the influence on it of the "idealistic and (in his eyes) priggish Shelley" (Buxton, 37). One only needs to read the following stanzas from the first canto of Byron's *Don Juan* (1819) to see that Shelley's ideas and ideals continued exercising Byron, despite the winningly performed quizzical aspect of the latter's attitude:

> Young Juan wander'd by the glassy brooks,
>   Thinking unutterable things; he threw
> Himself at length within the leafy nooks
>   Where the wild branch of the cork forest grew;
> There poets find materials for their books,
>   And every now and then we read them through,
> So that their plan and prosody are eligible,
> Unless, like Wordsworth, they prove unintelligible.
>
> He, Juan (and not Wordsworth), so pursued
>   His self-communion with his own high soul,
> Until his mighty heart, in its great mood,
>   Had mitigated part, though not the whole
> Of its disease; he did the best he could
>   With things not very subject to control,
> And turn'd, without perceiving his condition,
> Like Coleridge, into a metaphysician.

Juan is really Shelley, and Byron admires him, and is fond of him, and identifies with him. At the same time Byron himself is ostentatiously careful to avoid the mystic byways leading to what he can only perceive as Wordsworthian or Coleridgean cul-de-sacs. But Byron's essential sympathy with Shelley is greater than many commentators have acknowledged. In the following stanza, Juan's (Shelley's) intense curiosity in all the phenomena of an age of wonder is interrupted and usurped so believably and naturally in the last line by a deeper, and more real, human reality – love:

> He thought about himself, and the whole earth,
>   Of man the wonderful, and of the stars,
> And how the deuce they ever could have birth;
>   And then he thought of earthquakes, and of wars,
> How many miles the moon might have in girth,
>   Of air-balloons, and of the many bars
> To perfect knowledge of the boundless skies;–
> And then he thought of Donna Julia's eyes.

When Byron sees the young man "Dissatisfied, nor knowing what he wanted", he affects to settle for being amusedly content to infer that neither "glowing reverie, nor poet's lay, / Could yield his spirit that for which it panted." After all, Shelley did once actually try mathematically to confirm Plato's claim, in the *Republic*, "that the just man lived 729 times more pleasantly than the tyrant and the tyrant 729 times more miserably." (Wroe, 49) Shelley is incapable of settling into the role of humorous commentator on life's absurdities – though he does admire how Byron can do this, and will even attempt it himself in 'Peter Bell the Third' (1819) and 'The Witch of Atlas' (1820). But Shelley's most haunting works have about them the deeper dissatisfaction of a poet who can find respite in nothing that is actually available to him. "I am one of those whom nothing will fully satisfy" (*Letters*, II, 153), he told his friend, the editor of the *Examiner*, Leigh Hunt, in 1819. On the one hand he is the part of us that knows that from beneath the surface of everyday life, the rhythms of an ontological pressure can override all our gnat-whining. On the other hand, there are moments when Shelley's writing represents, in pellucid beads of compassion, the predicament of we who whine:

> We look before and after,
>   And pine for what is not;
> Our sincerest laughter
>   With some pain is fraught;
> Our sweetest songs are those that tell of saddest thought.

('To A Skylark', 86-90)

As a seeker after truth, Shelley will continue to devote his life to a pursuit that even his esteemed friend Byron thinks is silly. The best treatment that a visionary writer can expect from his contemporaries is to be left alone, so that he can remain, as Shelley put it,

> hidden
> In the light of thought,
> Singing hymns unbidden
> Till the world is wrought
> To sympathy with hopes and fears it heeded not. ('To A Skylark', 36-40)

The perennial philosophy is the only philosophy that is said to be inborn in human beings, expressing the natural structure of the human mind: "the metaphysics that recognizes a divine Reality substantial to the world of things and lives and minds", as Aldous Huxley has put it in *The Perennial Philosophy* (1946). This explains its constant periodic reappearances:

> Poised by the flood, e'en on the height thou holdest,
> Thou mayst now learn how the full tide of power
> Ebbs to its depths. (*Hellas*, 847-9)

Its influence is evident in ancient civilizations such as China and Egypt, which remained highly cultured for thousands of years. The superior dialecticians of these countries contemplated the fundamental problems that concern all human beings: the nature of God, moral obligation, and the significance of life and death. The great perpetuator of this philosophy, or way of seeing things, was Plato, through whom it was preserved and transmitted in western culture. Shelley's friend and contemporary, Horace Smith (1779-1849), recalled the poet's reverence for Plato:

> His [Shelley's] principal discourse … was of Plato, for whose character, writings, and philosophy he expressed an unbounded admiration … On my confession that I could not manage so subtle a thinker in the original Greek, but that I possessed Dacier's translation, Shelley replied, "Then you have seen him by moonlight, instead of in the sunshine; the closeness of his logic and the splendour of his diction cannot be transferred into another language. (Buxton, 54)

The universal wisdom has been an occult or hidden source of inspiration to poets, mystics and prophetic writers for many centuries. The physician, traveller and astronomer, James Lind (1736-1812), introduced Shelley to Plato's *Phaedrus* and the *Symposium* during Shelley's last two years at Eton. At this time Plato was thought too subversive to be taught officially in schools or universities, so it was crucial to Shelley's development that the eccentric and radical Lind took him on as a protégé. If one does not know about Shelley's rapport with Plato's work, one will have only a dull sense about what on earth (or in heaven) he is taking about. The poet and scholar Kathleen Raine has said that Shelley "belonged to a world and a class in which a man of culture measured himself against the whole of knowledge – a knowledge still given its unity by the spiritual orientation of the civilization from which it had arisen." (*Defending Ancient Springs*, 141)

In the meantime at University College, Oxford in 1811, before authoring the many sustained expressions of neo-Platonism that would identify him, for good or ill, as a being of another element, Shelley certainly did attract the attention of contemporaries of consequence. One of them, the Reverend J. Walker, a Fellow of New College, entered the Oxford booksellers Munday and Slatter just minutes after 'The Necessity of Atheism' had gone on sale there (in March 1811). Walker immediately saw to it that all copies but one were burnt in the back kitchen. It is possible that another Shelley pamphlet, the *Poetical Essay on the Existing State of Things* (1811), received similar treatment there and then. Astonishingly, this pamphlet has been known about, but actually missing until 2006. H.R. Woudhuysen's article in the *Times Literary Supplement* (14 July 2006), 'A Shelley Pamphlet Come to Light', has offered some new insights concerning the political controversy around Shelley: the pamphlet was written in support of Peter Finnerty, the radical Irish journalist and supporter of the United Irishmen who was then serving an eighteen-month sentence in Lincoln Gaol for libel. In the Preface to the *Poetical Essay*, Shelley calls for "a total reform in the licentiousness, luxury, depravity, prejudice, which involve society" by "gradual, yet decided intellectual exertions". But Shelley's more outspoken lines on the subject of Lord Castlereagh (whom Finnerty accused of trying to silence him), and his views about colonial India and the monarchy surely made Shelley's expulsion from Oxford inevitable.

Shelley's father, Sir Timothy Shelley (1752-1844), was deeply upset about his son's behaviour and expulsion, but he would not be the last person to suffer as the poet evolved. It was in Shelley's highly strung and exceptional nature to be at odds with institutions, and he knew how to wield language in a way that would make those he despised run for cover. The "Clientism, patronage and borough-mongering" (Wroe, 17-18) which ran in the aristocratic Shelley family was already among the poet's unhappily formative thought-patterns as he set about criticising the lacework of privilege known as society:

Commerce has set the mark of selfishness,
The signet of its all-enslaving power,
Upon a shining ore, and called it gold;
Before whose image bow the vulgar great,
The vainly rich, the miserable proud,
The mob of peasants, nobles, priests and kings,
And with blind feelings reverence the power
That grinds them to the dust of misery. (*Queen Mab*, V, 53-60)

The Shelleys were connected to the Duke of Norfolk, the great local landowner. Shelley's grandfather, Sir Bysshe, had been the first baronet, and Shelley's father, Sir Timothy, inherited the title when Sir Bysshe died in 1815. Sir Timothy was an inoffensive man, an MP for Shoreham, and a moderate Tory. But the poet's "tameless, and swift, and proud" ('Ode to the West Wind', IV) character would not let him simply complete his education at his father's old college and then go into politics mildly and inoffensively like his father. He would say in a letter to his father that

> *Obedience* is in my opinion a word which should have no existence – you regard it as necessary. –
>   Yes, you can command it. The institutions of society have made you, tho' liable to be misled by passion and prejudice like others, the *Head of the family*; and I confess it is almost natural for minds not of the highest order to value even the errors whence they derive their importance. (*Letters*, I, 115)

He could become frantically impatient with the limitations he felt other people – or even the part of himself about which he was least proud – imposing upon him. Hogg said that Shelley "could follow no other laws than the golden law of doing instantly whatever the inclination of the moment prompted." (Peck, I, 170) The poet knew that human beings are trained to conceal from themselves all perceptions that do not assist them in their routine struggles. He knew perfectly well, for example, that exemplary Christian behaviour involved being at one's, or at any rate at *his*, worst, like sitting still in a stiff chair, keeping rigidly attentive to oneself and to 'being good' instead of to the miracles (of nature and imagination) that make up the spacious and beautiful experience of a life lived to the full:

> Thou knowest … that … among the haunts of humankind,
> Hard-featured men, or with proud, angry looks,
> Or cold, staid gait, or false and hollow smiles,
> Or the dull sneer of self-loved ignorance,
> Or other such foul masks, with which ill thoughts
> Hide that fair being whom we spirits call man … (*Prometheus Unbound*,
> III, iv, 36-45).

To live and work with such people entails an unavoidable infinity of unacknowledged self-sacrifices. Concentration of attention on oneself (the mote in one's own eye) in order to turn a blind eye (and the other cheek) to swaggering mediocrity seemed to Shelley to close vistas, and therefore to kill poetry:

> thy forgotten dream;
> A dream itself, yet less, perhaps, than that
> Thou call'st reality. (*Hellas*, 843-5)

He was prepared to forfeit a craven security in order to win back the wonder of life. He recognised in the Greek gods (whose stories he read for himself in the original Greek) the numinous principle which seemed to him absent from his country's prevailing religion. He absorbed the stories with the same impassioned delight as he handled chemistry sets and microscopes. His annoyance after an Oxford lecture on mineralogy, for example, was plain when he said that the lecturer talked "About stones! – stones, stones, stones; – nothing but stones! – and so drily. It was wonderfully tiresome." (Peck, I, 72-3) He witnessed placeman mediocrity preaching at its ease from within its inherited systems, and with its imposing facts (including facts about stones) – for Shelley, "not what we want to know" (*Letters*, II, 277) – and he knew that such complacency is incompatible with spiritual attainment: "The source of poetry is native and involuntary but requires severe labour in its development." (Rogers, 1)

In *Julian and Maddalo* (1818), Julian (based on Shelley himself) argues with Maddalo (based on Byron) about what human freedom is:

> It is our will
> That thus enchains us to permitted ill.
> We might be otherwise; we might be all
> We dream of happy, high, majestical.
> Where is the love, beauty and truth we seek,
> But in our mind? and if we were not weak,
> Should we be less in deed than in desire? (170-6)

The contrast between what we actually are and how much better we could be is intuited without inhibition, and expressed with the fierce release of a bomb. Such brightness and directness are characteristic of youth yet to be corrupted, but the common understanding is that they must be gone in time for youth's traditional transformation into gregarious and professional manhood. Shelley was profoundly restless in a university – and, indeed, in a country – where, whichever way he looked, he saw conscious oppression, unconscious oppression, and the tyranny of the unimaginative.

Influenced by Wordsworth as he wrote about his own past, Shelley would often be keen to show that Nature was his friend and teacher. The following passage from the Preface to *The Revolt of Islam* (1817) demonstrates Shelley's view of "an education peculiarly fitted for a poet, without which genius and sensibility can hardly fill the circle of their capacities":

> I have been familiar from boyhood with mountains and lakes and the sea, and the solitude of forests; Danger, which sports upon the brink of precipices has been my playmate. I have trodden the glaciers of the Alps, and lived under the eye of Mont Blanc. I have been a wanderer among distant fields. I have sailed down mighty rivers, and seen the sun rise and set, and the stars come forth, whilst I have sailed night and day down a rapid stream among mountains. I have seen populous cities, and have watched the passions which rise and spread, and sink and change, amongst assembled multitudes of men.

The last sentence of the above passage suggests that the poet preferred to appreciate humanity's terrible energies impressionistically. And in a notebook entry of 1821, his own personal need for non-inclusion in the actual stew of human beings' specific evils is clear:

> I would not be, that which another is –
> I would not be equal below above
> Anything human. I would make my bliss
> A solitude! (Wroe, 13)

Shelley's liberalism can flow and erupt in his poetry, but in his actual life he could appear less liberal, and the contradiction has made an easy target of him for some critics. In 1818-19, the experience of being in Naples was ruined for him by the "deformity & degradation" of its inhabitants (*Letters*, II, 488). Nonetheless, merely to call him misanthropic is not to understand him deeply enough. He wanted not just to defend his "healing paradise" ('Lines Written

Among the Euganean Hills', 355) from the prevailing vulgarity, but to help cure readers of spiritually debilitating "pain, and guilt" (345), and the other symptoms of the materialist ethos of the "polluting multitude" (356):

> They ... would change; and soon
> Every sprite beneath the moon
> Would repent its envy vain,
> And the earth grow young again. (370-3)

"Permit, therefore," he wrote in his *Essay on Christianity* in 1815, "the Spirit of this benignant Principle to visit your intellectual frame, or, in other words, become just and pure."

The poet's eagerness to re-examine the premises upon which civilization exists is a world away from the cynicism, dandyism and pessimism of later 'Romantic' writing. In his prose poem, 'One O'Clock in the Morning' (1862), Charles Baudelaire would define his need to lock himself alone in his room away from the "Horrible life! Horrible city!", and he would tell of his compulsion to "produce a few lines which will prove ... I am not the lowliest of men, that I am not inferior to those I despise!" Shelley, too, despised people, but his *raison d'être* was not the polishing to a perfect shine of an individual brand of contempt for humanity. His lifelong interest in healing, somehow, the underlying causes of what he found himself despising is what makes him great. In the following passage from the Preface to *The Revolt of Islam* the poet understands the woof of the post-Revolutionary era and the increasingly pessimistic warp woven upon it by influential writers:

> The French Revolution may be considered as one of those manifestations of a general state of feeling among civilized mankind, produced by a defect of correspondence between the knowledge existing in society and the improvement or gradual abolition of political institutions. The year 1788 may be assumed as the epoch of one of the most important crises produced by this feeling ... The revulsion occasioned by the atrocities of the demagogues and the reestablishment of successive tyrannies in France was terrible, and felt in the remotest corner of the civilized world ... Thus many of the most ardent and tender-hearted of the worshippers of public good have been morally ruined by what a partial glimpse of the events they deplored appeared to show as the melancholy desolation of all their cherished hopes.

Wordsworth comes to mind here. For Wordsworth, the early days of the French Revolution were intoxicating: "Bliss was it in that dawn to be alive, / But to be young was very heaven" (*Prelude*, 10, 693-4). But Wordsworth became disillusioned on seeing newly liberated citizens merely turning into tyrants themselves:

> And now, become oppressors in their turn,
> Frenchmen had changed a war of self-defence
> For one of conquest, losing sight of all
> Which they had struggled for; and mounting up,
> Openly, in the view of earth and heaven,
> The scale of Liberty. (*Prelude*, 10, 791-6)

Mary Wollstonecraft (1759-97) had already expressed a similar concern during the early phase of the French Revolution: "if the aristocracy of birth is levelled with the ground, only to make room for that of riches … the morals of the people will not be much improved by the change, or the government rendered less venal." (Peck, II, 46) In all systems of strict convention, hypocrisy is never far behind. Like Wollstonecraft and Wordsworth before him, Shelley would "read [Liberty's] doom" (*Prelude*, 10, 796), and feel "Vex'd inly … and sore" (*Prelude*, 10, 797):

> Hence gloom and misanthropy have become the characteristics of the age in which we live, the solace of a disappointment that unconsciously finds relief only in the wilful exaggeration of its own despair. This influence has tainted the literature of the age with the hopelessness of the minds from which it flows. (Preface, *The Revolt of Islam*)

This has something other than the hot and strong opinions of journalism and the ostentatiously unemotional nature of academic analysis. Journalists and their readers are symbiotically prejudiced, and academics argue (often while claiming not to) that institutions of Terror are/are not excusable.

Shelley would say in 'Stanzas Written in Dejection, Near Naples' that he had

> Nor fame, nor power, nor love, nor leisure.
> Others I see whom these surround –
> Smiling they live, and call life pleasure; –
> To me that cup has been dealt in another measure. (III)

In *Being Shelley: The Poet's Search for Himself* (2007), Ann Wroe has explored Shelley's double existence: the growing poet also grew into a man. The latter obligation entailed the oppressive proximity of ordinary (if ardently self-interested) people, and their collective need to obliterate individuality: "that common, false, cold, hollow talk / Which makes the heart deny the *yes* it breathes" (*Prometheus Unbound*, III, iv, 149-50). With its Anglican ethos, and its history of having continually stocked the country with men in whose company Shelley "found [his] language misunderstood, like one in a distant and savage land" ('On Love'), Oxford University was

> insipid to me, uncongenial with my habits of thinking.– I could not descend to common life. The sublime interest of poetry, lofty and exalted achievements, the proselytism of the world, the equalization of its inhabitants were to me the soul of my soul.– You can probably form some idea of the contrast exhibited to my character by those with whom I was surrounded. (*Letters*, I, 227)

It has to be said that Shelley dramatized his young adulthood as a heroic struggle against mediocrity and evil, including his family's mediocrity and evil:

> For in vain from the grasp of the Bigot I flee;
> The most tenderly loved of my soul
> Are slaves to his hated control.
> He pursues me, he blasts me! 'Tis in vain that I fly; –
> What remains but to curse him, – to curse him and die? ('Bigotry's Victim', IV)

Some time after his expulsion from Oxford, he accused his father of

> a cowardly, base, contemptible expedient of persecution: is it not enough that you have deprived me of the means of subsistence (which means recollect you *unequivocally* promised) but that you must take advantage of the defencelessness which *our* relation entails upon me, to *libel* me ... You have treated me *ill, vilely*. When I was expelled for atheism, you wished I had been killed in Spain. (*Letters*, I, 148-9)

In another letter (*Letters*, I, 155), he even accused his mother of having an affair with his friend Edward Fergus Graham (engaged to Shelley's sister Elizabeth at the time). As Paul Johnson says, "There seems to have been no factual basis at all for this terrible letter." (*Intellectuals*, 34-5) But the true basis for such a state of mind may be found in another letter that Shelley wrote to William Godwin (1756-1836) in January 1812, in which he said that "Passive obedience was inculcated and enforced in my childhood" (*Letters*, I, 227). To his family's cost, Shelley was exercising an inner-directedness to counteract his conditioning. Causing inevitable harm to those around him, he had begun to beat his beautiful, terrible wings: "I am accustomed to speak my opinion unreservedly ... language is given us to express ideas – he who fetters it is a BIGOT and a TYRANT" (*Letters*, I, 147).

Even his good friend Hogg would sometimes have preferred Shelley to speak more flatly and convincingly (as, say, a historian or a mineralogist might speak), and not always as the visionary poet forever formulating perceptions blurred and brushed by dreams and darkness: "He was altogether incapable of rendering an account of any transaction whatsoever, according to the strict and precise truth, and the bare naked realities of actual life." (Wroe, 7) In one of his letters to Godwin, Shelley was untruthful about the publication dates of *Zastrozzi* and *St. Irvyne* (*Letters*, I, 227), and claimed (again, surely untruthfully) that he had been "twice expelled" from Oxford (*Letters*, I, 228). The essayist William Hazlitt (1778-1830) certainly relished toying with the contemplation of the pale-handed poet's otherworldly requirements:

> Mr Shelley ... has a fire in his eye, a fever in his blood, a maggot in his brain, a hectic flutter in his speech, which mark out the philosophic fanatic. He is sanguine-complexioned, and shrill-voiced. As is often observable in the case of religious enthusiasts, there is a slenderness of constitutional *stamina*, which renders the flesh no match for the spirit ... The shock of accident, the weight of authority make no impression on his opinions, which retire like a feather, or rise from the encounter unhurt, through their own buoyancy ... There is no *caput mortuum* of worn-out, thread-bare experiences to serve as ballast to his mind; it is all volatile intellectual salt of tartar, that refuses to combine its evanescent, inflammable essence with any thing solid or any thing lasting ...

In portraying Shelley's inability to engage with the real world as a constitutional shortcoming, Hazlitt produced yet another brilliant, malicious piece of drollery about a fellow-writer. Hazlitt flattered those readers that would consider themselves more responsive than Shelley to the "weight" and "authority" of the 'real' world. Savouring his own "salt", Hazlitt can make his readers savour it too:

He [Shelley] strives to overturn all established creeds and systems: but this is in him an effect of constitution. He runs before the most extravagant opinions, but this is because he is held back by none of the merely mechanical checks of sympathy and habit. He tampers with all sorts of obnoxious subjects, but it is less because he is gratified with the rankness of the taint, than captivated with the intellectual phosphoric light they emit. ('On Paradox and Commonplace')

To pursue Hazlitt's metaphor, the "phosphoric light" that he blamed Shelley for being captivated by would end up captivating others. (As Coleridge once said, "A man of genius may securely laugh at a mode of attack by which his reviler, in half a century or less, becomes his encomiast.") Hence the emergence of the strange radiance around Shelley' name – a radiance that would linger in the collective imagination of his devotees eager to love the exiled figure, yet not fully aware of the nature of his achievement.

3

Some Unseen Power and Some Critics' Attitudes

i.

Richard Holmes' influential biography has unwoven the unsatisfactory impression of Shelley the "angel" believed in by generations of "Shelley lovers". The poet Sir Stephen Spender (1905-95) has called Holmes' *Shelley: The Pursuit* (1974) "The best biography of Shelley ever written", and Spender has effectively celebrated a long-awaited coming of common sense to Shelley, and Romantic, studies:

> The great emphasis that Mr Holmes lays on Shelley's politics, philosophy and social activities corrects the usual view of an extraordinarily idealized, ethereal, spiritualized kind of poetry combined with an extraordinarily incoherent life … He has taken the Shelley story out of the realm of myth and made it far more convincing and significant.

But "far more convincing and significant" to whom? Presumably, the mid-1970s readership to whose collective materialism Holmes' and Spender's antennae were keenly and capably attuned. One Shelley lover unmentioned in Holmes' biography is the poet Francis Thompson (1859-1907). Thompson had a kind of lucidity and an ardour for the divine in line with Shelley's before him, and Shakespeare's before Shelley, and Plato's before Shakespeare: "When we become conscious in dreaming that we dream, the dream is on the point of breaking; when we become conscious in living that we live, the ill dream is but just beginning." (Thompson, 29) In the *Republic*, Plato said that nothing in human affairs is worth any great anxiety (X, 604), and as Shankara the Hindu philosopher put it, "Like an image in a dream, the world is troubled by love, hatred, and other poisons. So long as the dream lasts, the image appears to be real, but on awakening it vanishes." (*Atma Bodha*)

Holmes is right to say that "Shelley was at no point completely converted to Platonism" (432): the poet's reading was too deep and wide to allow fanatical fixation on the productions of one mind, however great. As the last two lines of 'To Jane, the Recollection' tell us, "Less oft is peace in Shelley's mind, / Than calm in waters seen." (V) "Plato and Calderon have been my gods" (*Letters*, II, 245), he told his friend Thomas Love Peacock (1785-1866) in November 1820. "I read the Greek dramatists & Plato forever" (*Letters*, II, 364), he told John Gisborne (1770-1851) in October 1821. But despite the obvious presence in Shelley's thoughts of non-Platonic influences, Plato – the great perpetuator of the perennial wisdom inborn in human beings – does seem to have been Shelley's guiding light. Yes, as Holmes says, Shelley was "critical and comparative" and he "selected, disregarded and explored as he went" (432), but Shelley himself has put the issue of his spiritual orientation in a nutshell: "I had rather err with Plato than be right with Horace." (*Letters*, II, 75) It can be seen that Shelley's inheritance from the perennial wisdom – more *via*, than simply *from* Plato – facilitated his mystical vantage-point over the death of Keats (and over his own death perhaps):

> Peace, peace! he is not dead, he doth not sleep –
> He hath awakened from the dream of life –
> 'Tis we, who, lost in stormy visions keep
> With phantoms an unprofitable strife,
> And in mad trance strike with our spirit's knife
> Invulnerable nothings. *We* decay
> Like corpses in a charnel; fear and grief
> Convulse us and consume us day by day,
> And cold hopes swarm like worms within our living clay. (*Adonais*, XXXIX)

But the specifically Platonic lustre of the following lines is incontrovertible:

> The One remains, the many change and pass;
> Heaven's light forever shines, Earth's shadows fly;
> Life, like a dome of many-colored glass,
> Stains the white radiance of Eternity,
> Until Death tramples it to fragments. – Die,
> If thou wouldst be with that which thou dost seek!
> Follow where all is fled! – Rome's azure sky,
> Flowers, ruins, statues, music, words, are weak
> The glory they transfuse with fitting truth to speak. (*Adonais*, LII)

Though it contains no direct evidence of his awareness of the *philosophia perennis* or Plato's transmission of it as an actual source for Shelley, Francis Thompson's personal enthusiasm for Shelley is infectious. Thompson appreciates the poet's ability, and need, to skip the sort of petty details that lure most other writers into the run of the mill. (Shakespeare was uninterested in the casualty figures of the Battle of Bosworth when he wrote *Richard III*, and it is unlikely that Wordsworth counted his 10,000 daffodils.)

Shelley's assertion that "Nought may endure but Mutability" ('Mutability') is, again, in agreement with the Platonic conception of the eternal unchanging forms:

> We are as clouds that veil the midnight moon;
> How restlessly they speed, and gleam, and quiver,
> Streaking the darkness radiantly! – yet soon
> Night closes round, and they are lost forever ('Mutability').

The world of experience is illusory. Anyone with the time and inclination to still the blether of the conscious mind knows this. The conscious mind churns thoughts associated with money, pleasure, luxury, sex, and so on. Underneath all this are present the incomparably more sublime and meaningful archetypes (such as truth, justice and beauty), which have no figure, colour, magnitude or number – in fact no separate distinctive traits at all. Yet their power is eternal, invincible and undeniable, and can take possession of the mind that opens, and the heart that watches and receives, as Wordsworth said in his lyric poem, 'The Tables Turned' (1798).

As early as June 1811, Shelley had already begun providing people with directions to deeper reality. "You have read Locke," he told Elizabeth Hitchener, "– you are convinced that there are no innate ideas, & that you do not always think when asleep. Yet, let me enquire in these moments of intellectual suspension, do you suppose that the soul is annihilated[?]" (*Letters*, I, 116). Warming to the theme in this letter, Shelley shows that he can be inspired by philosophy in a way that does not clog the arterial flow of poetic vision:

> You cannot suppose [that the soul is annihilated during sleep], knowing the infallibility of the rule, '*From nothing, nothing can come, to nothing nothing can return*' – as by this rule it could not be annihilated, or if annihilated could not be capable of resuscitation. This brings me to the point. Those around the lifeless corpse are perfectly aware that *it* thinks not: at least they are aware that when scattered thro' all the changes which matter undergoes it cannot then *think*. You have witnessed *one* suspension of intellect in dreamless sleep – you witness another in Death. (*Letters*, I, 116)

By 1815, he was expressing his view of the interactivity between individual human beings and divinity:

> We live and move and think; but we are not the creators of our own origin and existence. We are not the arbiters of every motion of our own complicated nature; we are not the masters of our own imaginations and moods of mental being. There is a Power by which we are surrounded, like the atmosphere in which some motionless lyre is suspended, which visits with its breath our silent chords at will. (*Essay on Christianity*)

By 1816, he was contemplating the spectacle of Mont Blanc in the Vale of Chamouni and finding himself responsive to the great mountain's "voice … to repeal / Large codes of fraud and woe" ('Mont Blanc', III, 81). For the poet, the mountain's presence defines with peculiar emphasis the impostures of Christianity. The energy in the flux of phenomena gushes exhaustlessly from an ancient source, or as Byron – despite his so pointedly not classing himself as a Platonist – would call it, "the controlless core":

> The everlasting universe of things
> Flows through the mind, and rolls its rapid waves,
> Now dark, now glittering, now reflecting gloom,
> Now lending splendor, where from secret springs
> The source of human thought its tribute brings
> Of waters, – with a sound but half its own,
> Such a feeble brook will oft assume
> In the wild woods, among the mountains lone,
> Where waterfalls around it leap forever,
> Where woods and winds contend, and a vast river
> Over its rocks ceaselessly bursts and raves. ('Mont Blanc', I, 1-11)

Shelley was keen to conceptualise the fundamental energy of the "everlasting universe", whether it was driving the clouds in the sky or vivifying the waters and woods below, in the perennial master-context:

> this Whole
> Of suns, and worlds, and men, and beasts, and flowers,
> With all the silent or tempestuous workings
> By which they have been, are, or cease to be,
> Is but a vision; all that it inherits

Are motes of a sick eye, bubbles, and dreams;
Thought is its cradle and its grave, nor less
The future and the past are idle shadows
Of thought's eternal flight – they have no being;
Nought is but that which feels itself to be. (*Hellas*, 776-85)

It is perhaps reasonable now to reintroduce the point that Byron had little of Shelley's enthusiasm for Plato, as the following stanza from Canto I of *Don Juan* shows:

O Plato! Plato! you have paved the way,
  With your confounded fantasies, to more
Immoral conduct by the fancied sway
  Your system feigns o'er the controlless core
Of human hearts, than all the long array
  Of poets and romancers: – You're a bore,
A charlatan, a coxcomb – and have been,
At best, no better than a go-between.

Byron's outburst is free of real malice, and it also contains an admission of Plato's real achievement, as a "go-between", or an intermediary between the "core / Of human hearts" and the intellects at the tips of the finest poets' senses.

In the early nineteenth century, Platonism had found its way into some popular English reading habits (if not into schools and universities). 'Mr. Mystic', in Peacock's novel *Melincourt* (1817), was based on Thomas Taylor the Platonist, and Byron had a unique knack of mirroring to the bourgeois reading public the metastases of its latest pretensions. But Byron knew that Shelley was unique, and utterly free from pretension. Byron knew that although most Greek-less, self-professed Plato-enthusiasts probably found (even translations of) the *Phaedrus* and the *Symposium* hard work – or boring – for Shelley Plato was alive and as directly at work as he had been in his own day – a continually vitalising presence.

Professional scholars knew of the glaring defects in Taylor's translations; and in his own musings on Christianity and its academic and industrial concomitants, Taylor was incisive, inspirational, entertaining, and extravagantly tactless:

On all sides nothing of philosophy remains but the name, and this has become the subject of the vilest prostitution; since it is not only engrossed by the naturalist, chemist and anatomist, but is usurped by the mechanic in every trifling invention, and made subservient to the lucre of traffic and merchandise. There cannot surely be a greater proof of the degeneracy of the times than so unparalleled a degradation and so barbarous a perversion of terms ...

And again:

> To a genius, indeed, truly modern, with whom the crucible and the air-pump are alone the standards of Truth, such an attempt [to reveal truth] must appear ridiculous in the extreme. With these, nothing is real but what the hand can grasp or the corporeal eye perceives, and nothing useful but what pampers the appetite or fills the purse ... (from Taylor's Introduction to Plotinus' 'An Essay on the Beautiful').

However exhilarating Taylor's outspokenness might have been for an early nineteenth-century readership looking for books 'off the beaten track', no one – and least of all an autodidact and underdog like Taylor – was going to undo the materialistic ethos. But Taylor's marginalized zeal did inspire insights central to some of the greatest Romantic poetry ever written. Curiously, these insights are also central to the greatest problems of twentieth- and twenty-first-century physics:

> Since matter ... is neither soul, nor intellect, nor life, nor form, nor reason, nor bound, but a certain indefiniteness; nor yet capacity, for what can it produce? Since it is foreign from all these, it cannot merit the appellation of being, but is deservedly called non-entity. Nor yet is it non-entity in the manner as motion or station; but it is true non-entity, the mere shadow and imagination of bulk and the desire of subsistence; abiding without station, of itself invisible, and avoiding the desire of him who wishes to perceive its nature. Hence, when one perceives it, it is then in a manner present, but cannot be viewed by him who strives intently to behold it. Again, in itself contraries always appear, the small and the great, the less and the more, deficience and excess. So that it is a phantom, neither abiding nor yet able to fly away, capable of no one denomination and possessing no power from intellect, but constituted in the defect and shade, as it were, of all real being. Hence, too, in each of its vanishing appellations it eludes our search; for if we think of it as something great, it is in the meantime small; if as something more, it becomes less; and the apparent being which we meet with in its image is non-being, and as it were a flying mockery. So that the forms which appear in matter are merely

ludicrous, shadows falling upon shadow, as in a mirror, where the position of a thing is different from its real situation; and which, though apparently full of forms, possesses nothing real and true but imitations of being and semblances flowing about a formless semblance ... And since matter ... has no solidity they penetrate it without division, like images in water, or as if anyone should fill a vacuum with forms. (from Taylor's note 6 to Plotinus' 'An Essay on the Beautiful')

If the pursuit of truth was ever damned by excessively worldly educators, Taylor sought to redeem it. Such ideas as Taylor's, so antagonistic to the received view of the universe as a collection of lumps in space held together by the laws of science, helped Wordsworth, Coleridge, Blake, Shelley and Keats travel in golden realms of thought, dreams and poetry.

On reading chapter 3 of Mary Shelley's (1797-1851) *Frankenstein* (1818), one recognises in the brilliant and fiery young Victor Frankenstein something of a Thomas Taylor, or a Blake, or a Shelley, commencing a "Mental Fight" (to borrow Blake's words) against dispiriting compromise, hypocrisy and authoritarian impositions. A Frankenstein, a Taylor, a Blake or a Shelley will not cease until he has either built 'Jerusalem' or self-destructed:

"The ancient teachers of this science," said he [the conventional university lecturer employed to dispense the received wisdom of the day], "promised impossibilities and performed nothing. The modern masters promise very little; they know that metals cannot be transmuted, and that the elixir of life is a chimera ..." (*Frankenstein*, chapter 3).

Shelley's learning, like Victor Frankenstein's, belongs to the older European (pre-Enlightenment) civilization whose cognoscenti were less anxious to dismiss human hope, with all its beauty and force, as a non-existent "chimera". On listening to the professor's encomium on the newly authoritative figures of modern science, Frankenstein feels stirring in himself an impulse to oppose their Academy, even though the struggle will probably end in his own personal ruin:

Such were the professor's words – rather let me say such were the words of fate, enounced to destroy me. As he went on, I felt as if my soul were grappling with a palpable enemy ... So much has been done, exclaimed the soul of Frankenstein – more, far more, will I achieve ... I will pioneer a new way, explore unknown powers, and unfold to the world the deepest mysteries of creation.

Mary Shelley's Frankenstein is clearly based on her husband, who wrote his Dedication of *The Revolt of Islam* to her in 1817:

> And from that hour did I with earnest thought
> Heap knowledge from forbidden mines of lore;
> Yet nothing that my tyrants knew or taught
> I cared to learn ... ('To Mary', V).

It was from ancient wisdom dismissed by his contemporaries that Shelley, like Frankenstein, drew boldness and power, and with this wisdom the poet said things of fundamental importance to humanity. He had no interest in the personal destruction of aristocrats, nor indeed in continuing to be an aristocrat himself. Instead, he wanted to get people to think about the direction of human energy and whether it may not be better directed:

> I am not an aristocrat, or any *crat* at all but vehemently long for the time when man may *dare* to live in accordance with *Nature* & Reason, in consequence with Virtue – to which I firmly believe that Religion, it's establishments, Polity & it's establishments, are the formidable tho' destructible barriers.– (*Letters*, I, 116-17)

It is worth pausing to consider the scale of Shelley's ambition as a poet. He cared about humanity, he believed it could be better than it is, and he cared about producing work that would redound to humanity. These are cares that later poets have tended not to have.

With limited patience rather than opulent intuition, Stephen Spender has called Shelley "a highly over-spiritualized creature". Spender's (unwittingly?) ambiguous judgment seems in one way to square neatly enough with Leigh Hunt's view of Shelley as "one of the noblest of human beings ... who had more religion in his very differences with religion, than thousands of your church-and-state men" (*The Liberal*). But Spender, in accordance with the materialist premises of mid-twentieth-century England, has delivered a scrupulously secular report on a deeply spiritual poet. Spender can take the reader no further than his excellent education – including his respect for the canon – allows. Hence, for Spender, Shelley (who did it his way) is inferior to Milton (who did it His way, even though He did not exist in the collective attitude of the 1930s Oxbridge set to which Spender belonged). To be sanguine about the stifling propinquity of minor poets' verdicts on major poets, the former sometimes inadvertently reveal the boundless superiority of the latter.

What of Shelley's "differences with [institutionalised] religion" noticed by Hunt? Asked by Edward Trelawny why he remained complicit with his enemies in his identification as an atheist, Shelley answered:

> It is a word of abuse to stop discussion, a painted devil to frighten the foolish, a threat to intimidate the wise and good. I used it to express my abhorrence of superstition; I took up the word as a Knight took up a gauntlet, in defiance of injustice. The delusions of Christianity are fatal to genius and originality: they limit thought. (Peck, I, 112)

Marilyn Butler's contention that Shelley was an "atheist" (3) can be unhelpful. Even the intellectual vantage point reached by Shelley in his late teens throws in the shade much of the 'down to earth' terminology of twentieth-century Romantic studies: "*Atheism* appears a terrific monster at a distance; *dare* to examine it, look at it's companions, it loses half it's terrors ..." (*Letters*, I, 116). Francis Thompson, who knew and loved Shelley's work with a poet's osmosis of understanding, wished to help continue the transmission of the mystical vision:

> The universe is his box of toys. He dabbles his fingers in the day-fall. He is gold-dusty with tumbling amidst the stars. He makes bright mischief with the moon. The meteors muzzle their noses in his hand. He teases into growling the kennelled thunder, and laughs at the shaking of its fiery chain. He dances in and out of the gates of heaven: its floor is littered with his broken fancies. He runs wild over the fields of ether. He chases the rolling world. (*Shelley*, 45-6)

Anyone who has delighted in the 'Ode to the West Wind' – "Drive my dead thoughts over the universe / Like withered leaves to quicken a new birth!" (V) – may feel a fitness about Thompson's stratospheric rapport with the lyric poet at work. But in the end Thompson's delight enchants and exhilarates more than it illuminates. Pleasure in Shelley of the Thompson variety may induce too much forgetfulness of Aristotle's truism – "Man is a political animal" – from which the author of 'The Mask of Anarchy' and many other political poems is not exempt. Yes, Shelley's work is in kilter with a cosmogonic paradigm whose laws are real, but not material (like the laws of mathematics or music), and Thompson's grasp of Shelley's gold-dust and growling thunder is brilliantly instinctive. But throughout the essay Thompson's Catholic principles keep him disconnected from Shelley's Platonic source of power. Thompson's essay, so shot through with flashes of individualistic insight, runs solely on its author's fine, but finite, enthusiasm before its entropy. Now long since at rest and chopfallen, it has become an article of curiosity for the literary palaeontologist to stumble upon and perhaps classify. But better a faded rocket than never a burst of light.

Arthur Hugh Clough (1819-61) said that "Shelley made wings for other people to fly on." And for the young Robert Browning (1812-89) Shelley was a "Sun-treader". So two more eminent Shelley lovers could in a sense be seen as in league with Thompson in encouraging readers to 'over-spiritualise' Shelley. Even so, readers easily bored by terrestrial restrictions may find unexpected afflatus in some of the more earthbound accounts of Shelley. Hogg, who knew Shelley personally at Oxford, enumerated the contents of Shelley's university rooms, apparently leaving the pleasure of "tumbling amidst the stars" with the poet to others:

> Books, boots, papers, shoes, philosophical instruments, clothes, pistols, linen, crockery, ammunition, and phials innumerable, with money, stockings, prints, crucibles, bags, and boxes, were scattered on the floor and in every place. – The table, and especially the carpet, were already stained with large spots of various hues, which frequently proclaimed the agency of fire. An electrical machine, and an air pump, the galvanic trough, a solar microscope, and large glass jars and receivers, were conspicuous amidst the mass of matter. Upon the table by his side were some books lying open, several letters, a bundle of new pens, and a bottle of Japan ink, that served as an inkstand; a piece of deal, lately part of the lid of a box, with many chips, and a handsome razor that had been used as a knife. There were bottles of soda water, sugar, pieces of lemon, and the traces of an effervescent beverage. Two piles of books supported the tongs, and these upheld a small glass retort above an argand lamp. (Peck, I, 68)

From Hogg's account, the reader may glean a sense of the velocity and voluminosity of Shelley's sense of wonder. This would remind one of young Frankenstein's almost frenzied dedication to "unfold to the world the deepest mysteries of creation." It may be the case that Hogg, writing his *Life of Percy Bysshe Shelley* in 1858, is remembering his friend through the prism of Mary Shelley's *Frankenstein* and some fragments of her projected life of Shelley:

> He [Shelley] proceeded, with much eagerness and enthusiasm, to show me [Hogg] the various instruments, especially the electrical apparatus: turning round the handle very rapidly, so that the fierce, crackling sparks flew forth; and presently standing upon the stool with glass feet,

he begged me to work the machine until he was filled with the fluid, so that his long, wild locks bristled and stood on end. Afterwards he charged a powerful battery of several large jars; labouring with vast energy, and discoursing with increasing vehemence of the marvellous powers of electricity, of thunder and lightning; describing an electrical kite that he had made at home, and projecting another and an enormous one, or rather a combination of many kites, that would draw down from the sky an immense volume of electricity, the whole ammunition of a mighty thunderstorm: and this being directed to some point would produce the most stupendous results. (Peck, I, 68-9)

Hogg's account of Shelley may be usefully compared with Thompson's. For all Hogg's apparent lack of Thompson's deep-sky pursuit of the poet, Hogg still allows for the principium – which Shelley called "The awful shadow of some unseen Power" ('Hymn to Intellectual Beauty', I) – to operate beyond the solidity of the material details. The material details for Shelley (as for Plato, and for Wordsworth at his best) were in reality the shades of, or the symbols for, what is most important, and most real. Until he could reveal to a readership's consciousness what existence really is (and it really is *not* the product of the Christian God to whom, as Genesis has it, it all seemed like a good idea at the time), he would be obliged to be labelled an 'atheist', which he was not, as his 'Hymn to Intellectual Beauty' shows:

> I vowed that I would dedicate my powers
> To thee and thine – have I not kept the vow?
> With beating heart and streaming eyes, even now
> I call the phantoms of a thousand hours
> Each from his voiceless grave …
> They know that never joy illumed my brow
> Unlinked with hope that thou wouldst free
> This world from its dark slavery, –
> That thou, O awful Loveliness,
> Wouldst give whate'er these words cannot express. (VI)

Many of his other works show very clearly that he did not reject belief in a supreme being, or beings, eternal, spiritual, and transcendent. In *A Defence of Poetry* he shows that the poet makes the normally opaque screen of language into a transparent diaphragm, or a window into eternity: "Poets are the hierophants of an unapprehended inspiration; the mirrors of the gigantic shadows which futurity casts upon the present; the words which express what they understand not; the trumpets which sing to battle and feel not what they inspire; the influence which is moved not, but moves." The "divine order" and "the mind of the creator" make up the very nucleus of the poet's concerns. This is very much akin to the Platonic conception of "Muses" (*Letters*, II, 29). It is not for nothing that in *Prometheus Unbound* Shelley has Demogorgon insist to Asia that God made the world.

Marilyn Butler, whose book, *Romantics, Rebels & Reactionaries* (1981), "would influence thinking about the Romantics for years to come" (*Byron Journal*), has laconically rehearsed a general impression of Shelley along the lines of Matthew Arnold's, Richard Holmes' and Stephen Spender's accounts of the poet:

> Shelley has not been the same man in our century since posterity in his own transformed him into Ariel: beautiful, ethereal, with the waves washing or the wind blowing through his hair.
>
> From the start, the notion of the poet as rebel was a generous one. Along with the flamboyant Byronic model it could accommodate something more manageable, the sensitive individual who rejected worldliness, and even, literally, this vulgar material world for a better.

Butler's dryness implies the acceptance of rigorous standards, submission to ascertainable facts, and the aspiration of historiography towards the status of an exact science – as if Shelley had not authored *A Defence of Poetry*, *Prometheus Unbound* and the 'Hymn to Intellectual Beauty': "Readers who were religious idealists – and there were many of these in the 1830s and 1840s – soon found it possible to forget the inconvenient Shelleyan atheism in this congenial otherworldliness." (Butler, 3) 'Atheism' is not the only "inconvenient" aspect of Shelley, and he knew this, and played up to it. He wrote to John Gisborne in October 1821: "As to real flesh & blood, you know that I do not deal in those articles, – you might as well go to a ginshop for a leg of mutton, as expect anything human or earthly from me." (*Letters*, II, 363) Symptoms of spiritual and imaginative ignorance were (and of course still are) everywhere, especially in learned society. Shelley's "words which express what they understand not" are not necessarily more futile than those of Christianity:

> … the names of Demon, Ghost and Heaven,
> Remain the records of their vain endeavor –
> Frail spells … ('Hymn to Intellectual Beauty', III).

The poet and vicar Robert Herrick (1591-1674) had formulated 'What God Is' with a muscular simultaneity of succinctness and expansiveness: "God is above the sphere of our esteem, / And is the best known, not defining Him." Herrick lived in a time before there was routine pressure on poets (and their reviewers) –or, rather, on reviewers (and their poets) – to pay court to a nineteenth-century readership with an appreciable proportion of self-satisfied churchgoers. Butler is right to note that Shelley's era saw an unprecedented proliferation of newspapers and magazines. This was at the beginning of the age of industrial-strength literary criticism, an era (which has continued to exist and gain in strength to this day) in which reviewers got paid to froth into ideologically appropriate sound-bites their analyses of the latest published works. Shelley understood the position and resolved to 'go down with his ship' – "Mr. Shelley is unfortunately but too well known for his infamous novels and poems. He openly professed himself an atheist" (*The Gentleman's Magazine*) – putting his trust in the propensity of his deepest values for finding their way through, eventually, to an appreciative readership. This is why he exhorted the west wind to

> Drive my dead thoughts over the universe
> Like withered leaves to quicken a new birth!
> And by the incantation of this verse,
>
> Scatter, as from an unextinguished hearth
> Ashes and sparks, my words among mankind!
> Be through my lips to unawakened earth
> The trumpet of a prophecy! ('Ode to the West Wind', V)

The poet's chief concern involved his expressing, for the benefit of mankind, a "harmonious madness" ('To A Skylark', 103), which is arguably more separate from pathology than the sanity and common sense of school inspectors, professional biographers and university professors. Writing to Peacock in August 1818, Shelley would commend specifically "a wonderful passage ... in [Plato's] *Phaedrus* ... in praise of poetic madness, and in definition of what poetry is, and how a man becomes a poet." (*Letters*, II, 29) The passage Shelley has in mind is Socrates' speech:

> There are several kinds of divine madness. That which proceeds from
> the Muses taking possession of a tender and unoccupied soul,
> awakening, and bacchically inspiring it towards songs and other poetry,
> adorning myriads of ancient deeds, instructs succeeding generations;

but he who, without this madness from the Muses, approaches the poetical gates, having persuaded himself that by art alone he may become sufficiently a poet, will find in the end his own imperfections, and see the poetry of his cold prudence vanish into nothingness before the light of that which has sprung from divine insanity. (*Letters*, II, 29)

Shelley effectively describes how he himself has coped as a marginalized figure:

Every man who lives in this age and desires to write poetry, ought, as a preservative against the false and narrow systems of criticism which every poetical empiric vents, to impress himself with this sentence [quoted above from *Phaedrus*] (*Letters*, II, 29-30).

And so Shelley's consciousness of his possessing (or being possessed by) an exulted imagination as intense as, and corresponding to, the finest of antiquity would drive him to write *Queen Mab* (1813), and from there through to *The Triumph of Life* (1822).

He is uncompromising in his belief that we can and should be better than we are, according to our birthright as human beings:

Man is of soul and body, formed for deeds
Of high resolve; on fancy's boldest wing
To soar unwearied … (*Queen Mab*, IV, 154-6).

There are echoes in this of Hamlet, lingering over an ideal even as he is aware at some level that the outward events of life are carrying him towards madness (of the pathological, non-Platonic variety), maturity, mediocrity, middle-age, or some other dreary burial-place where high hopes are so often put to rest: "What a piece of work is a man, how noble in reason, how infinite in faculties, in form and moving how express and admirable, in action how like an angel, in apprehension how like a god: the beauty of the world, the paragon of animals!" (*Hamlet*, II, ii) Man (for Shakespeare "this quintessence of dust") is, for Shelley, all too often

formed [by corrupt society] for abjectness and woe,
To grovel on the dunghill of his fears,
To shrink at every sound, to quench the flame
Of natural love in sensualism, to know
That hour as blest when on his worthless days
The frozen hand of death shall set its seal,
Yet fear the cure, though hating the disease. (*Queen Mab*, IV, 159-65)

Shelley retains and renews his disgust for a society that actually creates, preserves and rewards professional weaklings:

> Then grave and hoary-headed hypocrites,
> Without a hope, a passion or a love,
> Who through a life of luxury and lies
> Have crept by flattery to the seats of power,
> Support the system whence their honours flow. (*Queen Mab*, IV, 203-7)

Many people are, of course, proficient at bottling their finer feelings, and undertaking ambitious, practical careers based on material, quantifiable results or rewards: "Falsehood demands but gold to pay the pangs / Of outraged conscience" (*Queen Mab*, V, 197-8). Such people make up a substantial proportion of the labour force on whose votes the political parties depend for their existence and power:

> manhood tamely does
> His bidding, bribed by short-lived joys to lend
> Force to the weakness of his trembling arm.
> They rise, they fall; one generation comes
> Yielding its harvest to destruction's scythe.
> It fades, another blossoms; yet behold!
> Red glows the tyrant's stamp-mark on its bloom,
> Withering and cankering deep its passive prime.
> He has invented lying words and modes,
> Empty and vain as his own coreless heart;
> Evasive meanings, nothings of much sound,
> To lure the heedless victim to the toils
> Spread round the valley of its paradise. (*Queen Mab*, IV, 224-36)

Manipulative politics is all about having people face away from, and never towards, their own needs. In the inner space of the imagination – which for Coleridge was "a repetition in the finite mind of the infinite I AM" – symbolism holds sway over the syllogisms devised by tyrants to make us work for them, and end up actually wanting to be owned by them. Shelley knows that symbolism is antecedent to language. The child with his teddy bear – or the 'childish' Shelley with his little paper boats (Holmes, 42, 65) – weaves whole worlds of 'illusion' that can end up enriching what the world calls real. Blake had already said as much in his 'Proverbs of Hell' (1793): "What is now proved was once only imagin'd." Humphry Davy's safety lamp did not spontaneously appear. Neither did the system of levers and pulleys used to transport miners up and down the mine. The French Revolution could not have occurred without the thoughts and dreams that gave rise to it. Print could not have come about without someone's neurons first firing up an idea. And, as Hazlitt once said, the French Revolution was the remote but inevitable outcome of the invention of print. There is the rub. What realities may come when one has fed the hungers of the mind? Frankenstein provides one answer (a creature driven to meaningless violence). Oppenheimer provides a variation (the A-bomb). Shelley's more unusual answer bursts into hope in the receptive reader's mind, rather than exploding into the actual, murderous flames with which inventors of the literal kind have created Hell on earth.

ii.

The Revolt of Islam would have nothing to do with Islam but much to do with "kindling within the bosoms of my readers a virtuous enthusiasm for ... liberty and justice," as Shelley says in the poem's Preface. His skylark "never wert" a bird – indeed "What thou [the skylark] art we know not" – but it has about it the attributes of a bearer of news arrived out of the dark. Shelley's bird, like Keats' urn or Wordsworth's daffodils, is located on a frontier between outward impressions and inward legibility. Only in the rarefied air of such a frontier is the poet enabled to raise the flame that will weld the waking and the dreaming mind; and so it is with something of the skylark's "harmonious madness" that the poet sees into the heart of a very human need – and in seeing it he feels even more strongly the need to be at a distance from the ideological dialectic of materialism:

> 'The iron rod of penury still compels
> Her wretched slave to bow the knee to wealth,
> And poison, with unprofitable toil,
> A life too void of solace to confirm
> The very chains that bind him to his doom ... (*Queen Mab*, V, 127-31).

His hatred of the machismo that causes war is justly and solidly present, both in the main text of *Queen Mab* itself and in his own notes to the poem. In the notes, war's wrongness seems more wrong in juxtaposition with the mystery of the cosmos:

> That which appears only like a thin and silvery cloud streaking the heaven is in effect composed of innumerable clusters of suns, each shining with its own light and illuminating numbers of planets that revolve around them. Millions and millions of suns are ranged around us, all attended by innumerable worlds ...

> To employ murder as a means of justice is an idea which a man of an enlightened mind will not dwell upon with pleasure. To march forth in rank and file, and all the pomp of streamers and trumpets, for the purpose of shooting at our fellowmen … to inflict upon them all the variety of wound and anguish; to leave them weltering in their blood; to wander over the field of desolation, and count the number of the dying and the dead, – are employments which in thesis we may maintain to be necessary, but which no good man will contemplate with gratulation and delight.

To this day, such powerful views are habitually regarded as 'simplistic' by producers and consumers of media in warlike nations. *Queen Mab* has been babbled into existence as utterances that any competent reactionary could easily write off as political baby talk:

> 'War is the statesman's game, the priest's delight,
> The lawyer's jest, the hired assassin's trade,
> And to those royal murderers whose mean thrones
> Are bought by crimes of treachery and gore,
> The bread they eat, the staff on which they lean. (*Queen Mab*, IV, 168-72)

One decidedly competent reactionary, Paul Johnson, has said that from Shelley's teens, his

> approach to politics was coloured both by his taste for secret societies and by the conspiracy theory of history preached by the Abbé [Barruel, author of *Memoirs Illustrating the History of Jacobitism* (1797-98), which had put the blame for society's ills at the feet of the Illuminati, the Masons, the Rosicrucians and the Jews] and his kind. He could never shake it off, and it effectively prevented him from understanding British politics or the motives and policies of men like Liverpool and Castlereagh, whom he saw merely as embodied evil. (Johnson, 32)

Johnson makes the arresting point that "some of Shelley's acquaintances [including Peacock] never saw his politics as anything more than a literary joke, a mere projection into real life of Gothic romance." But Johnson has absorbed from Holmes' "superb" (Johnson, ix) biography the insights of pathology, and remained impervious to Shelley's Platonism. Johnson has learned from Holmes that Shelley's fantasies sometimes "came near to hallucinations" (Holmes, 113), and that

The outlet for his [Shelley's] own tension, found in the tendency to terrorize his feminine companions, has been noted from his earliest childhood. The themes of ghosts and hauntings were endemic to his poetry, providing a powerful source of private imagery, which reflected his alienation from the society around him. Moreover, the imaginative investigation of these abnormal states in himself and in others, conducted almost in the spirit of the psychologist, had a permanent fascination for him ... (Holmes, 114).

The fact that Plato is not mentioned once in Johnson's essay is an excellent little illustration of the ubiquity of Psychology and Psychiatry, and the dearth of Philosophy and Poetry, in twentieth-century letters. Already diminished by the time the Romantics were writing (or why would they have written with such vehemence?), philosophy and poetry have since been diminished even more, to the point that

> Like a star in heaven
> In the broad daylight
> Th[ey] ar[e] unseen ('To A Skylark', 18-20).

A true poet can remain attuned to the least possibility of the miraculous, even in an era dismissive of such a frequency. The skylark is only *temporarily* out of sight until it comes down again near enough to be seen. The "star in heaven" is only *temporarily* undetectable by the eye until the paradoxically illuminating fall of night. The real riches in poetry can only be *temporarily* obscured by, say, an 1810s commitment to utility, or an 1860s concern about propriety, or 1930s Oxbridge left-ism, or late-twentieth-century psychoanalytic theories, or whatever other mode of discourse happens to be mushrooming in the space between poetry and people who should read it.

"Circumstances meant so little to him," as Arthur Symons has said, "that he was unconscious of the cruelty of change of sentiment, and thus of the extent of his cruelty to women. He aimed at moral perfection, but was really of a perfect aesthetic selfishness." (Peck, I, 371) Undoubtedly, Shelley the man was driven by the urges that stir any male with such remorseless triviality. The suicide in 1816 of his first wife, Harriet Shelley (née Westbrook), and his marriage that December to Mary Wollstonecraft Godwin, suggests that Shelley's sorrow as a widower was not as strong as his impulse to pursue his happiness as a lover. However, one thing might be of prevailing importance to those who don't need geniuses to be nice people: Shelley was motivated in his writing by what is finest and noblest in humanity. "Our most imperial and stupendous qualities," he says,

– those on which the majesty and power of humanity is erected – are, relatively to the inferior portion of its mechanism, active and imperial; but they are the passive slaves of some higher and more omnipotent Power. This Power is God; and those who have seen God have, in the period of their purer and more perfect nature, been harmonized by their own will to so exquisite a consentaneity of power as to give forth divinest melody, when the breath of universal being sweeps over their frame. (*Essay on Christianity*)

Protesting that Shelley "has never had fair play", a reviewer in the *Paris Monthly Review* claimed that "His pen, when it was directed against his revilers, seemed to be guided by the hand of Love, and acrimonious expressions rarely fell from his lips." The point is a fair one, in that Shelley's love of Athenian democracy does, with maturity, outshine his hatred of the corruption of contemporary British life:

> But Greece and her foundations are
> Built below the tide of war,
> Based on the crystalline sea
> Of thought and its eternity;
> Her citizens, imperial spirits,
> Rule the present from the past;
> On all this world of men inherits
> Their seal is set. (696-703)

The idea expressed in the lines above, from *Hellas* (1821), is that the premise of a superior civilization is like an eternal rock "below" the shallower flux and reflux of conflict. Perhaps it should not be very surprising, then, that by the time he wrote *Hellas*, Shelley had moved away from Britain – bounded by her choppy seas and governed by her churchmanly falsifiers of experience – to the brightness of the Mediterranean. "I now understand," he told Peacock in January 1819,

> why the Greeks were such great Poets, & above all I can account, it seems to me, for the harmony the unity the perfection the uniform excellence of all their works of art. They lived in a perpetual commerce with external nature and nourished themselves upon the spirit of its forms. Their theatres were all open to the mountains & the sky. (*Letters*, II, 74)

He found a clarity in his isolation which, after all, brought him intimacy with places he hallowed more than Britain:

> Their [the ancient Greeks'] temples were mostly upaithric; & the flying clouds the stars or the deep sky were seen above. O, but for that series of wretched wars which terminated in the Roman conquest of the world, but for the Christian religion which put a finishing stroke to the antient system; but for those changes which conducted Athens to its ruin, to what an eminence might not humanity have arrived! (*Letters*, II, 74-5)

There is the suggestion in this letter that as a result of his mind-expanding reading and travel, Shelley has discovered a possible cause of the British narrowness and tyranny he detests so much: it is the remote yet inevitable outcome of roofs having been put over theatres and places of worship. This is not mere whimsy on Shelley's part. His belief seems to be that roofs on certain buildings block "the deep sky" and other manifestations of God from people's notice, and therefore from their habits of thinking. (Oscar Wilde would tell the Americans that their violence was inevitable because their wallpaper was so hideous, but Wilde knew better than Shelley how to smuggle seriousness through humorous customs.) One imagines the flat clever voice of Professor John Carey, the author of *What Good Are the Arts?* (2005), on the subject. Millers of public understanding like Carey and Dawkins are always on the lookout for grist, and only when it suits them are they responsive to the superior crackle of electricity from more sensitive (if sometimes wayward) thinkers. Hence the short mention of C.G. Jung (the Swiss gentleman who developed the concept of the collective unconscious) in Dawkins' *The God Delusion*: Dawkins notes only Jung's "belief that particular books on his shelf spontaneously exploded with a loud bang." Shelley, like Jung, is one of those thinkers out of whose allegedly silly sayings one could compile an anthology, for the chain book stores, with their outlets in thousands of glittering malls. These allegedly silly sayings, however, have their roots and contexts, serious investigations of which tend not to be found in anthologies. The idiosyncrasy, fascination, and naivety of Shelley's suggestion about roofs is characteristic of his life's work in setting up an alternative world-view and way of life. In his essay, *A Vindication of Natural Diet* (1812), he claimed that if Parisians in 1793 had been vegetarians, there would have been no Terror. If this idea too is, in the end, part of a grandiloquent fantasy, it also has a tincture of humanity, and even of the tragic sense that must go together with the Romantic ideal. Is it not hardhearted and ignorant to dismiss the idea without wandering with it, musing upon it, reflecting from it, bringing home to it, prophesying upon it, and dreaming upon it?

Away from Britain, Shelley finds more mental space and strength to be who he really is, and express what he really thinks. "I think I have an accession of strength since my residence in Italy" (*Letters*, II, 153), he told Hunt in November 1819. The parallel worlds, Britishness and Shelley's alternative, could not have inhabited the same space and time on speaking terms. The following extract is from an anonymous attack on *The Revolt of Islam* in the *Quarterly* (April 1819), at the time the most popular and influential review in Britain:

> Mr Shelley would abrogate our laws – this would put an end to felonies and misdemenours at a blow; he would abolish the rights of property, of course there could thenceforward be no violation of them … he would overthrow the constitution, and then we should have no expensive court, no pensions or sinecures … no army or navy; he would pull down our churches, level our Establishment, and burn our bibles … marriage he cannot endure, and there would at once be a stop put to the lamented increase of adulterous connections amongst us, whilst repealing the cannon of heaven against incest, he would add to the purity and heighten the ardour of those feelings with which brother and sister now regard each other; finally, as the basis of the whole scheme, he would have us renounce our belief in our religion … (Holmes, 544).

The *Quarterly* consistently and authoritatively expressed the British reactionary spirit, and John Taylor Coleridge (the author of the review) saw it as his duty to recognise evil and fight it with deadly seriousness (rather than allow readers to think Shelley was soft enough for a more playful lampooning):

> Like the Egyptian of old, the wheels of his chariot are broken, the path of mighty waters closes in upon him behind, and a still deepening ocean is before him: – for a short time are seen his impotent struggles against a resistless power, his blasphemous execrations are heard, his despair but poorly assumes the tone of triumph and defiance, and he calls ineffectually to others to follow him to the same ruin – finally, he sinks "like lead" to the bottom, and is forgotten. So it is now in part, so shortly will it be entirely with Mr Shelley. (Holmes, 544-5)

The hint of Shelley as an albatross around the neck of a nation that will slough him off ("like lead") into the sea looks amazingly prescient.

For contemporary English readers, Shelley was linked with Byron as part of the so-called Satanic school of poets. This term of abuse was coined by the then Poet Laureate Southey, for whom the two poets' attacks on establishment values were unconscionable:

... Men of diseased hearts and depraved imaginations, who, forming a system of opinions to suit their own unhappy course of conduct, have rebelled against the holiest ordinances of human society, and hating that revealed religion which, with all their efforts and bravadoes, they are unable entirely to disbelieve, labour to make others as miserable as themselves, by infecting men with a moral virus that eats into the soul! The school which they have set up may properly be called the Satanic school ... (Preface to *A Vision of Judgment*, 1821).

It seems that Shelley's 'atheism' hung around him like a dreadful aura, and as the brittle and pernickety reading-public flipped through its weekly papers, it would learn to despise, or fear, or simply continue not to know about the poet. Mrs Elizabeth Grant's account of Shelley at Eton and Oxford is redolent of the reasonableness (including the mechanical incredulity) instilled in people by conventional educators:

The ringleader in every species of mischief within our grave walls was Mr. Shelley, afterwards so celebrated, though I should think to the end half-crazy. He began his career by every kind of wild prank at Eton, and when kindly remonstrated with by his tutor, repaid the well-meant private admonition by spilling an acid over the carpet of the gentleman's study, a new purchase, which he thus completely destroyed. He did no deed so mischievous at University, but he was very insubordinate, always infringing some rule, the breaking of which he knew could not be overlooked. He was slovenly in his dress, and when spoken to about these and other irregularities, he was in the habit of making such extraordinary gestures, expressive of his humility under reproof, as to overset first the gravity, and then the temper, of the lecturing tutor. Of course these scenes reached unpleasant lengths, and when he proceeded so far as to paste up atheistical squibs on the chapel doors, it was considered necessary to expel him ... (Peck, I, 107).

Mrs Grant's account does not have much to say about how, or what, Shelley really thought.

In his essay, 'On Paradox and Commonplace', Hazlitt wished to show how immature (if not dangerous) Shelley was:

It would seem that [Shelley] wanted not so much to convince or inform, as to shock the public by the tenor of his productions, but I suspect he is more intent upon startling himself with his electrical experiments in morals and philosophy; and though they may scorch other people, they are to him harmless amusements, the coruscations of an Aurora Borealis, that play around the head, but do not reach the heart! Still I could wish he would put a stop to the incessant, alarming whirl of his Voltaic battery. (Holmes, 45)

Despite all the attacks from the left, right and centre, the reality is that Shelley wrote some of the greatest poetry in the English language.

In 1822, he would meet the death (seemingly foretold by J.T. Coleridge in the *Quarterly*) by drowning in his sailboat, the *Don Juan* (named after Byron's poem), during a storm off the Bay of Leghorn. Oddly, it looks as if he himself had anticipated the event in his poem, *Alastor*:

> The boat fled on, – the boiling torrent drove, –
> The crags closed round with black and jagged arms,
> The shattered mountain overhung the sea,
> And faster still, beyond all human speed,
> Suspended on the sweep of the smooth wave,
> The little boat was driven. A cavern there
> Yawned, and amid its slant and winding depths
> Ingulfed the rushing sea. The boat fled on
> With unrelaxing speed. – 'Vision and Love!'
> The Poet cried aloud, 'I have beheld
> The path of thy departure. Sleep and death
> Shall not divide us long.' (*Alastor*, 358-69)

According to Edward Trelawny, Shelley – impatient genius that he was – in effect mined pyramids of books in search of clues about life's meaning: "his eyes glistening with an energy as fierce as that of the most sordid gold-digger who works at a rock of quartz, crushing his way through all impediments, no grain of the pure ore escaping his eager scrutiny." (Peck, I, 77) Perhaps the impatience culminated, in the end, in a sort of clumsy experiment – a question that Shelley put to Nature, trying to force her to "render up the tale / Of what we are." (*Alastor*, 28-9) Shelley's final experiment – if that is what it was – involved the destruction of the very consciousness putting the question and awaiting the answer. Again, this puts one in mind of Hamlet, who is prepared to speak with the ghost "though hell itself should gape / And bid me hold my peace." (I, ii) And again, it puts one in mind of Victor Frankenstein, determined "to procrastinate all that related to my feelings of affection until the great object, which swallowed up every habit of my nature, should be completed." Or (to recognise an equivalent to Shelley in the literature of antiquity he knew so well) like Sophocles' Oedipus who, determined to find out his fate, pursued his enquiry, even when he knew that something appalling awaited him in the answer. Shelley did not give way to the Jocasta in the heart that the rest of us give way to. How fitting, then, that Shelley had a copy of Sophocles in his pocket when he died.

Yes, he did attack, say, in *Queen Mab*, "the slavish priest [who] / Sets no great value on his hireling faith" (V, 198-9). Yes, he did produce some discardable polemics on the subject of organised religion: "How ludicrous the priest's dogmatic roar!" (*Queen Mab*, VI, 64). But even during the hangover occasioned by the consumption of much Gothic fiction, his ability to lay bare the perniciousness of the opinion-mongers of his day is sobering, and uplifting:

> The weight of his [the priest's] exterminating curse
> How light! and his affected charity,
> To suit the pressure of the changing times,
> What palpable deceit! (*Queen Mab*, VI, 65-8).

The dispenser of the "exterminating curse", also the possessor of protean "charity", is "the priest" in Shelley's era, but it could just as easily be the hireling reviewer of any era since.

Shelley's life was short, but he finessed his spiritual orientation at such a rate that by his late twenties he was "defeat[ing] the curse which binds us to be subjected to the accident of surrounding impressions". He most valued the supernal elevation with which Platonic writers such as Dante and Shakespeare could see humanity's animal instincts at work *and* the divine context in which humanity has its place. Privileged by the parallax, he has helped readers to revisit history, geography, or, in the case of 'Ode to Heaven' (1820), theology:

> Thou [Heaven] art but the mind's first chamber,
> Round which its young fancies clamber,
>   Like weak insects in a cave,
> Lighted up by stalactites;
>   But the portal of the grave,
> Where a world of new delights
>   Will make thy best glories seem
>   But a dim and noonday gleam
> From the shadow of a dream!

The charge of otherworldliness has been levelled at the poet, but it is this world that the reader can revisit and reconsider through Shelley's writings because Shelley dared to see this world differently. Since that fateful time at Oxford when he lit a blue touch paper, he rapidly matured past the conflagration, and wrote a Revolution not as doctrine but "In the depths of the dawn" (*Prometheus Unbound*, IV, 4). With poetic sensitivity like heliotropism, he releases the sensation of a new beginning to the roots of posterity. He liberates readers with the feeling of hope, and with the further feeling that it is right to hope. Through Shelley, one learns of a sunrise that has to be believed to be seen.

4

Analyses of Some Major Poems

i. *Queen Mab: A Philosophical Poem* (1813)

The twenty-one-year-old Byron had run, head down, at many targets in his poem, *English Bards and Scotch Reviewers* (1809). Byron had been ridiculed in some of the reviews of his previously published book of poems, *Hours of Idleness* (1807), and the personal grievance was no doubt involved in the generation of his acerbity. By contrast, the force of Shelley's *Queen Mab* – including the poet's distaste for

> Those gilded flies
> That, basking in the sunshine of the court,
> Fatten on its corruption! (III, 106-8) –

is not so much the product of a personal desire to get even as it is the voice of the frank and naive speculator singling out the rickety palaces to be razed before Jerusalem can be built. If one thinks of the way Shelley's aristocratic contemporaries might have felt about what he was doing, the following Turkish proverb could be helpful: "When the axe came into the woods, many of the trees said: 'At least the handle is one of us.'"

In a letter of 1811, Shelley had already recognised some key edifices of error in English society:

> Vile as aristocracy is, commerce, purse-proud ignorance & illiterateness is more contemptible. I still see Religion to be immoral – when I contemplate these gigantic piles of superstition, when I consider too the leisure for the exercise of mind, which the labor which erected them annihilated, I set them down as so many retardations of the period when truth becomes omnipotent.

He has seen the appalling sum total of wasted time brought about by commerce, religion and superstition, but he can weigh up also the mizzling insignificant items, the heart-breaking fractions, the endless subdivisions of misery, that provoke him:

> Very useless ornament, the pillars, the iron railings, the juttings of
> wainscot, & … the cleaning of grates are all exertions of bodily labor,
> which tho' trivial separately considered when united destroy a vast
> proportion of this valuable leisure – how many things could we do
> without, how unnecessary are *mahogany* tables silver vases, myriads of
> viands & liquors, expensive printing that worst of all. (*Letters*, I, 151)

The integrity of the poet is therefore far-reaching and thorough. It inhabits
Shelley's corpus like a God, or rather, the perceiving and presiding "Spirit of
Beauty" ('Hymn to Intellectual Beauty', II) whose sanction the poet continually
seeks. In such a context, he can assess, for example, the specific political issue
of social inequality like a tolerant and rational citizen:

> Nature rejects the monarch, not the man;
> The subject, not the citizen; for kings
> And subjects, mutual foes, forever play
> A losing game into each other's hands,
> Whose stakes are vice and misery. (*Queen Mab*, III, 170-4)

The plot of *Queen Mab* does not, in itself, look particularly impressive.
Mab, the omniscient queen of the fairies, is drawn in a magic car to the bedside
of Ianthe, a sleeping girl. Ianthe is taken on a fantastic trip. Mab shows her
what has gone wrong in the world in the past, and exhorts her to continue to
fight against tyranny:

> … thy will
> Is destined an eternal war to wage
> With tyranny and falsehood, and uproot
> The germs of misery from the human heart. (*Queen Mab*, IX, 189-92)

Mab then re-deposits Ianthe in her bed.

The author would be denigrated both for the poem's 'airy-fairy' moments
and the 'street-protest' republicanism of its main theme. Such a poem
contributes significantly to the contrast between familiar eighteenth-century
poetry (generally so accepting of the political order of things) and what is now
known as Romanticism. With a self-soothingly charitable glance at a country
churchyard in which underprivileged people were buried, Thomas Gray (1716-
1771), a favourite poet of young Shelley, had already contemplated, with formal
benevolence, the lower orders, and even included in his work some conjecture
concerning ne'er discovered labouring-class equivalents of Milton and Newton:

Let not Ambition mock their useful toil,
Their homely joys and destiny obscure;
Nor Grandeur hear, with a disdainful smile,
The short and simple annals of the poor …

Perhaps in this neglected spot is laid
Some heart once pregnant with celestial fire;
Hands that the rod of empire might have swayed,
Or waked to ecstasy the living lyre … ('Elegy Written in a Country Churchyard').

Wordsworth would perceive such showy open-mindedness to have become far off and apathetic during his lifetime, and he would respond with the cutting edge of his *Lyrical Ballads* (1798): it was undoubtedly new for a poet to write with such genuinely sympathetic appreciation of what it might be like to experience the (unjust) world as an 'Idiot Boy', or a 'Mad Mother', or the poor little girl in 'We Are Seven' who actually wins an argument against the well-off, educated adult narrator of the poem – the sort of self-assured (because conventionally schooled) gentleman who puts his trust in the authority of his reasoning and the contagiousness of his dullness. Wordsworth was neither patronising nor sentimental in 'We Are Seven', but he seemed to imply that the girl, and by further implication her class, were fluent in a sort of wisdom which was simultaneously enlightening and unsettling for the well-heeled elite.

However, just over a decade after Wordsworth's quiet revolution, Shelley cannot help but feel that Wordsworth has somehow gone astray since his *Lyrical Ballads*. Wordsworth's long poem, *The Excursion* (1814), contained Wordsworth's recollection of Joseph Fawcett (1758-1804) and John Thelwall (1764-1834) – French sympathisers he had known in the 1790s – as material for the failed revolutionary known as 'The Solitary'. Percy and Mary Shelley both read *The Excursion* in September 1814, and Mary recorded in her journal, "Much disappointed. He [Wordsworth] is a slave." (*Journal*, 15) Shelley would write 'To Wordsworth' (1816) in which he would sadly recollect that the once radical Wordsworth "stood / Above the blind and battling multitude", and that "In honoured poverty [Wordsworth's] voice did weave / Songs consecrate to truth and liberty." But now, no longer radical, Wordsworth has left Shelley "to grieve, / Thus having been, that [Wordsworth] shouldst cease to be." As a result of the grievance, Shelley is even more inclined to press harder, fuelled by his flagrant imperative, and continually reorienting himself in relation to the principals that Wordsworth has abandoned: "truth and liberty."

Shelley's work has none of Gray's *soupçon* of formalism, and none of

Wordsworth's patience for gentle levelling and political gradualism. Shelley's highest achievements have been viewed unsympathetically, or uncomprehendingly, by those grounded in conformist premises:

> Power, like a desolating pestilence,
> Pollutes whate'er it touches; and obedience,
> Bane of all genius, virtue, freedom, truth,
> Makes slaves of men, and of the human frame
> A mechanized automaton. (*Queen Mab*, III, 176-80)

He cannot, however, be compared with any authenticity to, say, Robespierre, whose hatred of intransigence and mendacity in both friend and foe led to his misapplying his mind in his pursuit of democracy with such atrocious results. Shelley's work is resolvable into one ingredient – love – and the absence of another – fear. He knows that most readers' tastes are regulated by a culture that promotes the absence of the former and the presence of the latter. So he knows that his real achievement is going to be sealed off from most readers and, as it were, in a never-never land, through a looking glass, in a dimension parallel to the one the world calls real. "Time is our consciousness of the succession of ideas in our own mind," he said in one of his notes to *Queen Mab*, "Thus the life of a man of virtue and talent, who should die in his thirtieth year, is with regard to his own feelings longer than that of a miserable priest-ridden slave who dreams out a century of dullness." Most people remain (or are kept) unaware that there could exist any deeper reality from which phenomena (armchairs, earthworms, blue silk-pantaloons and red revolutionary berets) flourish. There are, for example, many Shelley enthusiasts unlikely to recognise in the poet's work anything other than the scorch-marks of fiery political radicalism – the verbal arson of a talented barbarian.

Shelley argues that although "every heart contains perfection's germ" (*Queen Mab*, V, 147), the modern money-worshipping way of life is "Blunting the keenness of ... spiritual sense / With narrow schemings and unworthy cares" (*Queen Mab*, V, 162-3). *Queen Mab* has been called "the most revolutionary document of the age in England" (Christiansen, 49), but some years after writing it Shelley would find himself worried by the poem. Perhaps the poet's anxiety about a work now extant – at large, even – and beyond his control found its way into Mary Shelley's depiction of Victor Frankenstein's troubles. Frankenstein recalled that after the "infinite pains and care [he] had endeavoured to form [his creation]", and until just the split-second before he succeeded in "infus[ing] a spark of being into" it, he had remained insensible of the misery awaiting him on the successful completion of his task. But from the moment the creature opened its dull yellow eye and breathed hard, Frankenstein found himself exiled forever from personal comfort or happiness, and it was the *autonomy* of the thing he had created – the actual embodiment of many fears, unexamined and discarded, but now returning to him in ghastly majesty – that shook him through so hard:

> His [the monster's] limbs were in proportion, and I had selected his features as beautiful. Beautiful! – Great God! His yellow skin scarcely covered the work of muscles and arteries beneath; his hair was of a lustrous black, and flowing; his teeth of a pearly whiteness; but these luxuriances only formed a more horrid contrast with his watery eyes, that seemed almost the same colour as the dim white sockets in which they were set, his shrivelled complexion and straight black lips.

As a young man, Shelley wished that he could transmute the "withered leaves" of deciduous human hopes into an evergreen and graspable ideal. He wanted the sum force of his imagery and symbolism – carried on his rhythms of syntactic patterns and semantic complexes, and focussed by the many other elements of his discourse – to infuse his work with soul, or "to quicken a new birth!", as he would put it in the 'Ode to the West Wind'. He would find out something important about the personal cost involved in making a significant contribution to – and therefore really tampering with – the arrangement of the intellectual universe. *Queen Mab* – "written by me," said Shelley, "at the age of eighteen, I dare say in a sufficiently intemperate spirit" (*Letters*, II, 304) – was used against him at the trial which resulted in his losing custody of his children. The poem became a backdrop against which Shelley would be brought into disrepute by his enemies. *Queen Mab* backfired on Shelley a little like *The Picture of Dorian Gray* would backfire on Wilde, and, for that matter, like Frankenstein's creation would backfire on Frankenstein: "I had desired it with an ardour that far exceeded moderation; but now that I had finished, the beauty of the dream vanished, and breathless horror and disgust filled my heart."

In the early 1790s, Britain's foremost conservative theorist, Edmund Burke (1729-97), knew what he was talking about when he called the new French Republic a "strange, nameless, wild, enthusiastic thing". He had in mind the crowd – the rushing mob – on the streets of Paris, many-headed and pullulating, its component units seeming scarcely human and its aggregate lacking any noble features, its only language a roar. The "withered leaves" of Shelley's writings could easily become the fodder of the latest politicised 'monster', on whose palate the perennial and Platonic niceties would be lost. Even for years after Shelley's death, *Queen Mab* was an important influence on working-class radicals. In an accidental way similar to that of alchemists discovering gunpowder or the laws of gravity in their search for gold, Shelley created a monster in his search for something else.

There are two kinds of poetry lover: those who love it because it answers to their longing for beauty and wonder, and those who love it principally for its meaning. It has been possible for socialists to approve of Shelley's adolescent and vague political idealism, and to accept the poet's entranced lovers sailing in their magic boats. In *Red Shelley* (1980), Paul Foot has valiantly attempted to enlist the poet as an honorary socialist. But for socialist readers of Shelley, the message of the 'Ode to the West Wind' is the harnessing of the "impetuous one" in the cause of oppressed people. It is arguably a variation of Christianity that has been for many readers the new birth to be quickened. This was not the revolution Shelley had in mind. He really wanted to point out how far short of its potential society fell, his hope being that people might do something about it. In doing so, he found it absolutely necessary to vent some strong feelings and leave, for the attention of hireling reviewers, the incriminating singe marks on his labours:

> All things are sold: the very light of heaven
> Is venal; earth's unsparing gifts of love,
> The smallest and most despicable things
> That lurk in the abysses of the deep,
> All objects of our life, even life itself,
> And the poor pittance which the laws allow
> Of liberty, the fellowship of man,
> Those duties which his heart of human love
> Should urge him to perform instinctively,
> Are bought and sold as in a public mart
> Of undisguising Selfishness, that sets
> On each its price, the stamp-mark of her reign.
> Even love is sold; the solace of all woe
> Is turned to deadliest agony, old age
> Shivers in selfish beauty's loathing arms,
> And youth's corrupted impulses prepare
> A life of horror from the blighting bane
> Of commerce; whilst the pestilence that springs
> From unenjoying sensualism, has filled
> All human life with hydra-headed woes. (*Queen Mab*, V, 177-96)

If Shakespeare criticised, he did it obliquely. Prospero's magic can afford to be the rougher for its being practised on an island far, far from London. King Lear can fall apart in front of a London audience because, really, he reigned only in the remote past. *Queen Mab*, however, seems too transparent for its author's own good, and the poet is exhaling grievances in the bell jar of contemporary British politics. It will be a while longer before he will provide access to "the wonder of our deep being" with the sustained focus that renders untenable the view of him as no more than a tub-thumper.

ii. *Alastor or The Spirit of Solitude* (1815)

Mary Shelley said that

> *Alastor* is written in a very different tone from *Queen Mab*. In the latter, Shelley poured out all the cherished speculations of his youth – all the irrepressible emotions of sympathy, censure, and hope, to which the present suffering, and what he considers the proper destiny of his fellow-creatures, gave birth. *Alastor*, on the contrary, contains an individual interest only. A very few years, with their attendant events, had checked the ardour of Shelley's hopes …

The poem tells the story of a young man who dies yearning for the woman he met in his dreams, for whom he can find no earthly match:

> … He dreamed a veiled maid
> Sate near him, talking in low solemn tones.
> Her voice was like the voice of his own soul … (*Alastor*, 151-3).

The poem's epigraph, from Saint Augustine's *Confessions* (Book III, Chapter 1), shows Shelley's awareness that he is not the first person to have been troubled by the presence in him of strong feelings and the absence of an external object corresponding to those feelings: "I was not yet in love, but I was in love with love itself; and I sought for something to love, since I loved loving."

There is something enclosed about the spirit in which this poem was written. The elusive love interest floats above the poet like a pale ectoplasm, and its wavering existence seems to be drawn from each exhalation of the sleeping head. Shelley told Thomas Medwin about his dream journal:

> At this time Shelley was ever in a dreamy state, and he told me he was in the habit of noting down his dreams. The first day he said, they amounted to a page, the next to two, the third to several, till at last they

constituted the greater part of his existence … One morning he told me he was satisfied of the existence of two sorts of dreams, the Phrenic and the Psychic; and that he had witnessed a singular phenomenon, proving that the mind and soul were separate and different entities – that it had more than once happened to him to have a dream, which the mind was pleasantly and actively developing; in the midst of which, it was broken off by *a dream within a dream* – a dream of the soul, to which the mind was not privy; but that from the effect it produced – the start of horror with which he waked – must have been terrific. (*The Life of Percy Bysshe Shelley*, 89)

Shelley has become his own phantom, and is at once the haunting spirit and the haunted man:

> His strong heart sunk and sickened with excess
> Of love. He reared his shuddering limbs, and quelled
> His gasping breath, and spread his arms to meet
> Her panting bosom: – she drew back awhile,
> Then, yielding to the irresistible joy,
> With frantic gesture and short breathless cry
> Folded his frame in her dissolving arms.
> Now blackness veiled his dizzy eyes, and night
> Involved and swallowed up the vision; sleep,
> Like a dark flood suspended in its course,
> Rolled back its impulse on his vacant brain. (*Alastor*, 181-91)

His prose fragment 'On Love', contemporaneous with *Alastor*, shows a developing fascination with whatever mental agency sorts the scenes of life into the categories of alien and familiar, and sorts the feelings of life into the categories of attraction and repulsion: "It is that powerful attraction towards all that we conceive, or fear, or hope beyond ourselves, when we find within our own thoughts the chasm of an insufficient void and seek to awaken in all things that are a community with what we experience within ourselves." The lonely figure in *Alastor* is forced into the waking cold, rather like the narrator of Keats' 'La Belle Dame sans Merci' (written in 1819) finding himself "Alone and palely loitering" on "the cold hillside":

> Roused by the shock, he started from his trance –
> The cold white light of morning, the blue moon
> Low in the west, the clear and garish hills,
> The distinct valley and the vacant woods,
> Spread round him where he stood. (*Alastor*, 192-6)

The political animal that gave birth to *Queen Mab* can no longer merely be accused of bleeding quite so unwisely in a shark-filled sea.

Alexander Solzhenitsyn has since asked a question which (although not specifically meant to) encapsulates the contradiction that drove Shelley in directions as different as *Queen Mab* and *Alastor*: "If you desired to change the world, where would you start? With yourself or others?" On the one hand, *Queen Mab* makes it impossible for anyone who thinks not to notice that Shelley keeps scoring direct hits; the reader knows that certain things said in *Queen Mab* are true, because he flinches when he reads them. If one has any doubt about the reality of the poet's view on commerce, selfishness, unenjoying sensualism and hydra-headed woes, one has merely to look up from the page, switch on the television, and witness again for oneself the reality that the superior money, and language, is being hoarded and the inferior is dominating the circulation – the outward and obvious signs of Sir Thomas Gresham's (1519-79) law hard at work. On the other hand, *Alastor* encourages the reader to interrogate a specific (though hard to define) inner tension: how could the youth in the poem turn away from the greater love to the less, from his dream lover to a natural lover? How is it that the mortal sleep must fall upon the individual, even when he has glimpsed immortal beauty? And why?

> Whither have fled
> The hues of heaven that canopied his bower
> Of yesternight? The sounds that soothed his sleep,
> The mystery and the majesty of Earth,
> The joy, the exultation? His wan eyes
> Gaze on the empty scene ... (*Alastor*, 196-201).

Shelley is one of those individuals who is not allowed to forget. He is "Obedient to the light / That [shines] within his soul" (*Alastor*, 493-4), and he is tempted to live in mourning for something great, "That beautiful shape!" (*Alastor*, 211) that has been "Lost, lost, forever lost / In the wide pathless desert of dim sleep" (*Alastor*, 209-10), rather than cultivate, with Wordsworthian patience, an appreciation of lesser things in the light of common day:

And now his limbs were lean; his scattered hair,
Sered by the autumn of strange suffering,
Sung dirges in the wind; his listless hand
Hung like dead bone within its withered skin;
Life, and the lustre that consumed it, shone,
As in a furnace burning secretly,
From his dark eyes alone. (*Alastor*, 248-54)

The above lines tell of the listening look that poets have. Their nerves sensitise uniquely on the line that divides dreams from waking life and reality from reverie: "Those who are subject to the state called reverie feel as if their nature were dissolved into the surrounding universe, or as if the surrounding universe were absorbed into their being. They are conscious of no distinction." (Holmes, 298) Where are the borders? Poets listen *through* themselves and others at least as much as they listen *to* themselves and others. They can collapse their own personal self-centredness in order to reach out (and in) and seize something from the marvel of being. They are hypersensitive commuters on the infrastructure of echoes in inner (and outer) space. They long to free themselves from the hereditary restrictions of their own nervous systems. They long to transcend themselves. A letter from Shelley to Hogg (8 May 1811) suggests as much:

> Solitude is most horrible; in despite of the [lack of self-love] which perhaps vanity has a great share in, but certainly not with my own good will I cannot endure the horror the evil which comes to *self* in solitude … what strange being am I, how inconsistent, in spite of all my bo[a]sted hatred of self – this moment thinking I could so far overcome Natures law as to exist in complete seclusion, the next shrinking from a moment of solitude, starting from my own company as it were that of a fiend, seeking any thing rather than a continued communion with *self* – Unravel this mystery – but no. I tell you to find the clue which even the bewildered explorer of the cavern cannot reach … (*Letters*, I, 77-8).

Dictated by a frantic and obscure compulsion, the poet creates the great cry that must go up from time to time from the heart of human nature. Individuals each carry the accumulating personal suffering about with them in their limbic systems, and most of them do not know how to communicate that suffering. Many of them will not cry out to something outside them, that is, they will not try to pray, because they worry that they will find again only the depth inside, where the instincts writhe and wriggle without intermission, and without hope.

Shelley expertly inspects the various cells in the mental prison-system of human nature:

> Those who, deluded by no generous error, instigated by no sacred thirst of doubtful knowledge, duped by no illustrious superstition, loving nothing on this earth, and cherishing no hopes beyond, yet keeping aloof from sympathies with their kind ... have their apportioned curse. They languish because none feel with them their common nature. They are morally dead ... (Preface, *Alastor*).

Having read Wordsworth's *Excursion* before writing *Alastor*, Shelley perceived that "self-centred [Wordsworthian] seclusion" leads to "the vacancy of ... spirit ... mak[ing] itself felt." In order to transcend "the lasting misery and loneliness of the world", Shelley sought to unite the blind, confused and fragmentary elements of universal experience within the sacred circle of significance sadly vacated by Wordsworth. He knew that supreme open-spiritedness was vital in order to assimilate and retain the "things [that] depart which never may return: / Childhood and youth, friendship and love's first glow", which all flee "like sweet dreams leaving [the dreamer] to mourn." ('To Wordsworth') For Shelley, Wordsworth's earlier work had been permeated with the wisdom of a fundamentally affectionate intellect, but *The Excursion* now revealed an unfortunate absence of that wisdom. Shelley knew that the poet's supreme task of synthesis – how to invoke the welding flame – could be taught and learned only by himself.

The poet recreates the youth's rapt inwardness –

> Oh, that the dream
> Of dark magician in his visioned cave,
> Raking the cinders of a crucible
> For life and power, even when his feeble hand
> Shakes in its last decay, were the true law
> Of this so lovely world! (*Alastor*, 681-6) –

but the poet also knows the light of common day that will disinterestedly excoriate the dreamer on his return:

> But thou art fled,
> Like some frail exhalation, which the dawn
> Robes in its golden beams, – ah! thou hast fled! (*Alastor*, 686-8)

The poet diagnoses solitary idealism as the root of an unhappiness that is in himself and rife in Britain (assuming in the latter, national form an insularity that considers anything not the product of British effort to be a sort of moral lapse). In order to examine it, Shelley has involved himself productively with the sort of self-indulgence and narcissism avoided so evidently by other poets prouder of their plain living and high thinking. We do owe much to Wordsworth. His best poetry has not aged. His clear eye that sees Tintern Abbey sees more than ours do, even if there are (as Huxley so astutely pointed out, in 1929, in 'Wordsworth in the Tropics') walls which it cannot see through, and which now can be seen from the other side of time. Shelley was already beginning to see from the other side of time. For him, Wordsworth's choice to see in Nature a divine, Anglican unity was like the big bang of yet another false universe which (as it has turned out) would become densely populated by Wordsworthians. One key Wordsworthian, Matthew Arnold, would write, in an essay on Byron, that Shelley was a "beautiful but ineffectual angel, beating in the void his luminous wings in vain". For the Professor of Poetry at Oxford (1857-62), the "incurable fault" of Shelley's poetry was its "insubstantiality". But what would 'curable' poetry from Shelley have been?

Shelley's challenge was always to keep his judgement, and to keep his language from being clouded by his anger. He knew that most people – including the eminent and ageing Wordsworth – cultivate heartfelt associations with parts, not the whole of life. He knew that these parts are fetishes – "Commerce" (*Queen Mab*, V, 53), "Obedience" (Wroe, 19), or "stones, stones, stones; nothing but stones!" (Peck, I, 72) – or as Thomas Taylor would have called them, "phantoms of false enthusiasm", invariable particularities which furnish hell on earth. Wordsworth's memory, once his greatest resource, would become his worry. Coleridge's over-developed self-analytical habits are legendarily masochistic:

> For not to think of what I needs must feel,
>   But to be still and patient, all I can;
> And haply by abstruse research to steal
>   From my own nature all the natural man –
>   This was my sole resource, my only plan:
> Till that which suits a part infects the whole,
> And now is almost grown the habit of my soul. ('Dejection: An Ode', VI)

Shelley's sympathy with the plight of a fellow visionary ensnared by the contingencies of life's surface appearances is moving:

Ah! wherefore didst thou build thine hope
On the false earth's inconstancy?
Did thine own mind afford no scope
Of love, or moving thoughts to thee?
That natural scenes or human smiles
Could steal the power to wind thee in their wiles. ('To Coleridge')

The author of *Alastor* is feeling the full burden of existence, and he is paying the psychic cost involved in assembling the disparate rags of experience when life's terrible energies are blowing around and through him, and when "faithless smiles" and "falsehood" ('To Coleridge') are pervasive in society. He tries to realise on paper his existence. So what if the author of *Alastor* is egotistical and self-absorbed? The point is that he has grasped something hard to define, yet ultimately definite, and he has the uplifting sense of having against great odds saved something from eternity. To make that something touchable, or to render it visible – whatever *it* is – will always seem to the majority of readers a vain task. As the professor says in C.S. Lewis' *The Lion, the Witch and the Wardrobe* (1950), "I wonder what they *do* teach them at these schools." (chapter 5) Maddeningly, for the poet also, the resumption of normal consciousness is too often accompanied by the painful sense of vanity, a pain that would provoke Arthur Rimbaud (1854-91) to abjure his art, and Hart Crane (1899-1932) to take his own life (and Wordsworth to write the politically self-correcting *Excursion* and *Peter Bell*). The poet's exaltation must fade away, and the moment must become immersed again in its customary insipidity: "The glory of the moon is dead; / Night's ghosts and dreams have now departed" ('To Coleridge'). Shelley knows well enough that his soaring birds, blasting trumpets, surging and breaking waves, howling and driving storms, and erupting volcanoes will be, *even to him sometimes, as well as to his harshest critics*, questionable fragments, trickeries, fantasies and guesses leaving him bored, leaving him awake, and leaving him alone. He knows that an important part of what he wants to say is neither resistant nor palpable, and that the unsettling absence of edges around it can push poets into insanity or send them back to the 'safer' regions (really, though, fetishes) of naturalistic description or correct politics. Shelley's poetry carries the echoes and harmonies of greater things, and though the concluding lines of *Alastor* concede that there are concrete reasons for pessimism, something between those lines is the uplift of a mood music most people thought was lost in the dissonance and bloodshed in Paris between 2 and 6 September 1792:

> Art and eloquence,
> And all the shows o' the world, are frail and vain
> To weep their loss that turns their lights to shade.
> It is a woe "too deep for tears," when all
> Is reft at once, when some surpassing Spirit,
> Whose light adorned the world around it, leaves
> Those who remain behind, not sobs or groans,
> The passionate tumult of a clinging hope;
> But pale despair and cold tranquillity,
> Nature's vast frame, the web of human things,
> Birth and the grave, that are not as they were. (710-20)

He knows that "the deep truth is imageless", and that he has a real poet's work to do, not just in translating deep, imageless truth into images, but in keeping and conveying, somehow, the fructifying spirit of the encounter:

> Oh! there are spirits in the air,
> And genii of the evening breeze,
> And gentle ghosts, with eyes as fair
> As starbeams among twilight trees ...
>
> With mountain winds, and babbling springs,
> And mountain seas, that are the voice
> Of these inexplicable things,
> Thou didst hold commune, and rejoice
> When they did answer thee ... ('To Coleridge').

iii. *The Revolt of Islam,* 1818 (originally *Laon and Cythna,* 1817)

During Shelley's schooldays at Eton (1804-10),

> The particular name of some particular boy would be sounded by one, taken up by another and another, until hundreds echoed and echoed the name ... The Shelley! Shelley! Shelley! which was thundered in the cloisters was but too often accompanied by practical jokes, – such as knocking his books from under his arm, seizing them as he stooped to recover them, pulling and tearing his clothes, or pointing with the finger, as one Neapolitan maddens another. The result was ... a paroxysm of anger which made his eyes flash like a tiger's, his cheeks grow pale as death, his limbs quiver, and his hair stand on end. (Holmes, 20)

Despite the environment unpropitious to learning, Shelley's hatred of tyranny, intensified by his first-hand exposure to it, spurred him to learn things tyrants did not know:

> Yes, from the records of my youthful state,
> And from the lore of bards and sages old,
> From whatso'er my wakened thoughts create
> Out of the hopes of thine aspirings bold,
> Have I collected languages to unfold
> Truth to my countrymen; from shore to shore
> Doctrines of human power my words have told;
> They have been heard, and men aspire to more
> Than they have ever gained or ever lost of yore. (*Revolt of Islam*, IV, xii)

This epic poem (at nearly 5000 lines, the longest Shelley ever wrote) is not about Islam. It is about revolution. In the introductory Dedication to his wife, Shelley recalls the moment when, as a schoolboy, he realised what he was supposed to do with his life:

> I do remember well the hour which burst
> My spirit's sleep. A fresh May-dawn it was,
> When I walked forth upon the glittering grass,
> And wept, I knew not why; until there rose
> From the near school-room voices that, alas!
> Were but one echo from a world of woes –
> The harsh and grating strife of tyrants and of foes. ('To Mary', iii)

One must understand Shelley in a non-literal way: it is unlikely that school lessons took place at "dawn" at Eton or Syon House. He is not lying. As Peacock said, "His imagination often presented past events to him as they might have been, not as they were" (Wroe, 7):

> And then I clasped my hands and looked around,
> But none was near to mock my streaming eyes,
> Which poured their warm drops on the sunny ground –
> So without shame I spake: – 'I will be wise,
> And just, and free, and mild, if in me lies
> Such power for I grow weary to behold
> The selfish and the strong still tyrannize
> Without reproach or check.' I then controlled
> My tears, my heart grew calm, and I was meek and bold. ('To Mary', iv)

At Eton, Shelley may or may not have hit back against one of the bullies by stabbing him with a fork – or perhaps a knife, depending on which of his accounts one believes (Holmes, 20) – but by his mid-twenties, in writing *Laon and Cythna*, he was hitting out at the establishment with sustained and concentrated radical force:

> For me the world is grown too void and cold,
> Since hope pursues immortal destiny
> With steps thus slow – therefore shall ye behold
> How Atheists and Republicans can die;
> Tell your children this! (XII, 30)

But many passages like this had to be diluted as a result of Shelley's consultation and compromise with his nervous publisher, Ollier. The fourth line of the above excerpt became "How those who love, yet fear not, dare to die", which is lamentably obscure by comparison. The re-worked poem, *The Revolt of Islam*, lost many of its more piquant political passages, and modified its underlying tolerance of incest, as the loss of the stanza beginning with the following lines shows: "I had a little sister, whose fair eyes / Were loadstars of delight, which drew me home" (*Laon and Cythna*, II, xxi).

In the Preface, Shelley explains his choice of the Spenserian stanza, a form he will use again in *Adonais* (1821):

> I have adopted the stanza of Spenser (a measure inexpressibly beautiful) not because I consider it a finer model of poetical harmony than the blank verse of Shakespeare and Milton, but because in the latter there is no shelter for mediocrity; you must either succeed or fail.

He has something to prove, both to himself and to "those whom I now address":

> This perhaps an aspiring spirit should desire. But I was enticed also by the brilliancy and magnificence of sound which a mind that has been nourished upon musical thoughts can produce by a just and harmonious arrangement of the pauses of this measure.

He means to somehow mimetically represent the eternal fugue from which the ceaselessly fluctuating temporal world issues. Neville Rogers' *Shelley at Work: A Critical Study* (1967) justly makes much of the fact that the manuscript drafts of Shelley's poems show a musical composer as much as a poet at work.

Even after the editorial work Shelley was obliged to do in order to get the poem published, there is still considerable power in *The Revolt of Islam*. Shelley is forceful enough about the poem's political purpose in the Preface: "the awakening of an immense nation from their slavery and degradation to a true sense of moral dignity and freedom; the bloodless dethronement of their oppressors and the unveiling of the religious frauds by which they had been deluded into submission". In the Preface, the prose is beautiful and powerfully flowing, and it feels in kilter with the convulsions of the French Revolution and its sequent wars:

> It has ceased to be believed that whole generations of mankind ought to consign themselves to a hopeless inheritance of ignorance and misery because a nation of men who have been dupes and slaves for centuries were incapable of conducting themselves with the wisdom and tranquillity of freemen so soon as some of their fetters were partially loosened.

There is something persuasive and even addictive about the poet's impetuosity, and, further, his way of raising and navigating the swells of rhetoric that seem to come through him from the "master-theme of the epoch" – the French Revolution: "There is a reflux in the tide of human things which bears the shipwrecked hopes of men into a secure haven after the storms are past. Methinks those who now live have survived an age of despair." He investigates the very poetic machinery with which he sends the sparks of his individuality into the universal imagination, which he trusts will be combustible:

> I have sought to enlist the harmony of metrical language, the ethereal combinations of the fancy, the rapid and subtle transitions of human passion, all those elements which essentially compose a poem, in the cause of a liberal and comprehensive morality; and in the view of kindling within the bosoms of my readers a virtuous enthusiasm for those doctrines of liberty and justice, that *faith and hope in something good, which neither violence nor misrepresentation nor prejudice can ever totally extinguish* among mankind. (italics added)

During the narration of the spiritual and sexual union of brother-and-sister lovers Laon and Cythna, one senses the ache, not just for flesh, but for something deeper, beyond materiality, of which the flesh is just a symbol:

> The Meteor showed the leaves on which we sate,
> And Cythna's glowing arms, and the thick ties
> Of her soft hair which bent with gathered weight
> My neck near hers; her dark and deepening eyes,
> Which, as twin phantoms of one star that lies
> O'er a dim well move though the star reposes,
> Swam in our mute and liquid ecstasies;
> Her marble brow, and eager lips, like roses,
> With their own fragrance pale, which Spring but half uncloses.
>
> The Meteor to its far morass returned.
> The beating of our veins one interval
> Made still; and then I felt the blood that burned
> Within her frame mingle with mine, and fall
> Around my heart like fire; and over all
> A mist was spread, the sickness of a deep
> And speechless swoon of joy, as might befall
> Two disunited spirits when they leap
> In union from the earth's obscure and fading sleep. (VI, xxxiii–xxxiv)

But the poem does sprawl in many different other directions, and fails to achieve the uniformity of impression that distinguishes, say, Milton's *Paradise Lost* (in which the sensual, the sexual, the spiritual and the political are made somehow to achieve the synergism of a single, epic insight from the other side of time). *The Revolt of Islam* is a repository for many of Shelley's personal and public interests at the time. The poem is (like *Queen Mab*) influenced by Godwin's *Political Justice* (1793), the key left-wing book of the time, including Godwin's hatred of all forms of tyranny. Shelley explores the more personal nature of the relationship between himself and the older political thinker:

> A course precipitous, of dizzy speed,
> Suspending thought and breath; a monstrous sight!
> For in the air do I behold indeed
> An Eagle [Godwin] and a Serpent [Shelley] wreathed in fight: –
> And now relaxing its impetuous flight,
> Before the aëreal rock on which I stood,
> The Eagle, hovering, wheeled to left and right,
> And hung with lingering wings over the flood,
> And startled with its yells the wide air's solitude. (I, viii)

The poem has affinities with Edmund Spenser's *Faery Queene* (1590-96). Like Spenser's, Shelley's descriptions are not picturesque, but they are more like dreams in their independence from specific geographical, historical or political realities. Shelley, like Spenser, puts nothing in the poem, not even the concept of the French Revolution, without keeping about it the frisson of the unknown from which dreams and actual events alike emerge:

> Thus, the dark tale which history doth unfold
> I knew, but not, methinks, as others know ...
> So that when Hope's deep source in fullest flow,
> Like earthquake did uplift the stagnant ocean
> Of human thoughts, mine shook beneath the wide emotion.
>
> When first the living blood through all their veins
> Kindled a thought in sense, great France sprang forth,
> And seized, as if to break, the ponderous chains
> Which bind in woe the nations of the earth. (I, xxxviii-xxxix)

Shelley has some of Godwin's rationalist belief in the benevolence of mankind, and he shares Godwin's wish to sweep away the restraints of social institutions, but he has in addition something of the Spenserian touch (such as unobtrusive but intentional alliterativeness helping to conjure hard-to-paraphrase dreamscapes) that had already reached Milton's *Paradise Lost* and Coleridge's 'Rime of the Ancient Mariner'.

Shelley also keeps the frisson of the unknown into which all must return:

> We know not where we go, or what sweet dream
> May pilot us through caverns strange and fair
> Of far and pathless passion, while the stream
> Of life our bark doth in its whirlpools bear ... (VI, xxix).

His short poem, 'Death', posthumously published by his wife in 1824, appears to be a balder statement of the problem:

> Death is here, and death is there,
> Death is busy everywhere,
> All around, within, beneath,
> Above, is death – and we are death ...

First our pleasures die – and then
Our hopes, and then our fears – and when
These are dead, the debt is due,
Dust claims dust – and we die too.

All things that we love and cherish,
Like ourselves, must fade and perish;
Such is our rude mortal lot –
Love itself would, did they not.

In such a situation as this, as in the Thousand and One Nights, we (who must die) are left (in the meantime) with stories. Stories, of course, are made of words, and, as Shelley says, poets' "words unveil the permanent analogy of things by images which participate in the light of truth; but as their periods are harmonious and rhythmical, and contain in themselves the elements of verse; being the echo of the eternal music." (*A Defence of Poetry*) So all must depend on how the stories are told. That is, all must depend on poetry. Shelley tells *The Revolt of Islam* with gusto, in a Preface and 12 cantos with (unlike *Queen Mab*) no notes. The villain of the story is the Establishment, which (for example) in the poet's view denies men freedom as long as it denies women freedom:

Can man be free if woman be a slave?
Chain one who lives, and breathes this boundless air
To the corruption of a closed grave!
Can they whose mates are beasts, condemned to bear
Scorn, heavier far than toil or anguish, dare
To trample their oppressors? In their home
Among their babes, thou knowest a curse would wear
The shape of woman … (II, xliii).

It may seem difficult sometimes to disagree with Paul Johnson that evildoers are portrayed merely as embodied evil in *The Revolt of Islam* (and 'The Mask of Anarchy'):

The Tyrant peoples dungeons with his prey,
Pale victims on the guarded scaffold smile
Because they cannot speak …

But Shelley instructively appreciates the efficiency with which those in control parcel out the miseries that regulate the status quo, here to a recalcitrant journalist (like Peter Finnerty) languishing in a prison-cell, and there to an anonymous boy begging on the chartered streets,

> and, day by day,
> The moon of wasting Science wanes away
> Among her stars, and in that darkness vast
> The sons of earth to their foul idols pray,
> And gray Priests triumph, and like blight or blast
> A shade of selfish care o'er human looks is cast. (IX, xxiv)

Again, as Shelley put it in the notes of *Queen Mab*, the wrongness of the imposed and maintained order of things looks even more wrong in juxtaposition with the "vast" mystery of the cosmos. But in *The Revolt of Islam* at its best, the poet's continuing blend of rebellion and wonder finds expression in an impressive flow of Spenserian stanzas. The authority with which Shelley now handles the notoriously difficult Spenserian form frees him from the need for a supplementary commentary in the manner of *The Botanic Garden*. That is, since registering his debt to (Erasmus) Darwin, Shelley has evolved, despite (or because of) a political environment where "truth and liberty" are no longer vital forces in Wordsworth:

> This is the winter of the world; – and here
> We die, even as the winds of Autumn fade,
> Expiring in the frore and foggy air. –
> Behold! Spring comes, though we must pass, who made
> The promise of its birth ... (IX, xxv).

With the subtlety and strength of a martial artist, the poet uses tyranny's own weight against it, presenting a nightmare the reader will recognise has been burned into the dreaming brain by actual wrong governance:

> Famine, than whom Misrule no deadlier daughter
> Feeds from her thousand breasts, though sleeping there
> With lidless eyes lie Faith and Plague and Slaughter –
> A ghastly brood conceived of Lethe's sullen water. (X, xvii)

Shelley had seen for himself the appalling state of post-Revolutionary France in 1814. He wrote from France to Harriet Shelley in August 1814:

> We came 120 miles in four days. The last two days we past over the country that was the seat of war. I cannot describe to you the frightful desolation of this scene. Village after village entirely ruined & burned; the white ruins towering in innumerable forms of destruction among the beautiful trees. The inhabitants were famished; families once perfectly independent now beg their bread … No provisions, no accom[m]odation; filth, misery & famine everywhere. (*Letters*, I, 392)

He had even heard horrible stories about innocent people having to resort to prostitution and cannibalism:

> There was no corn – in the wide marketplace
> All loathliest things, even human flesh, was sold;
> They weighed it in small scales – and many a face
> Was fixed in eager horror then. His gold
> The miser bought; the tender maid, grown bold
> Through hunger, bared her scorned charms in vain … (X, xix).

In Shelley's vision, a nation's citizens have been tyrannised into insanity:

> It was not hunger now, but thirst. Each well
> Was choked with rotting corpses, and became
> A cauldron of green mist made visible
> At sunrise. Thither still the myriads came,
> Seeking to quench the agony of the flame
> Which raged like poison through their bursting veins;
> Naked they were from torture, without shame,
> Spotted with nameless scars and lurid blaines –
> Childhood, and youth, and age, writhing in savage pains. (X, xxi)

This is far from simplistic. The poet does retain his hope for society, but not in any context of foursquare republicanism, and certainly not to the beat of the busy tempo of the tall Parisian guillotine. The shadow of the guillotine (and of the gunman) has spindled across time from Burke all the way to the modern reactionary's ideological slit-window: if one squints just so, one might make out the continuum of left-wing malevolence lurking in widespread tolerance of thinkers from Rousseau to Sartre.

Nuances get lost in dogmatic definitions. If anything, the analysis of *The Revolt of Islam* offered by the first president of the Shelley Society, the Reverend Stopford Brooke, in *Naturalism in English Poetry* (1820), is more attuned to the poet's frustrated power and fragmented compactness:

> [Shelley] tried to be real and to embody with temperance his ideas on
> the progress of mankind, but was continually swept in spite of himself
> into an impassioned idealism and fury; but where, feeling himself lost
> and uncontrolled, he tried to get back again into temperance and reality,
> and only half succeeded, so that the poem is broken, unequal,
> unsatisfactory from want of unity of impression. (Peck, II, 42)

Despite the poet's distemper, the slaughter of the multitude at the gates of the
Golden City resonates uncannily with the use in England in 1817 of cavalry and
yeomanry to break up public meetings and subdue dissatisfaction.
Dissatisfaction expressed in print, such as Richard Carlile's (1790-1843)
working-class periodical, *The Republican*, was also vigorously checked. Carlile
would be tried for blasphemous libel in October 1819. The charge was based
on several passages in Paine's *Age of Reason*. For this, and also for the
republication of Palmer's *Principles of Nature*, Carlile was fined £1,500 and put
in Dorchester Gaol for three years. In a masterly letter to Hunt intended for
publication in the *Examiner*, Shelley showed that the authorities' sentencing of
Carlile was a symptom of their ingrained intolerance:

> the prosecutors care little for religion, or care for it only as it is the mask
> & the garment by which they are invested with the symbols of worldly
> power. In prosecuting Carlisle they have used the superstition of the
> Jury as their instrument for crushing a political enemy, or rather they
> strike in his person at all their political enemies. They know that the
> Established Church is based upon the belief in certain events of a
> supernatural character having occurred in Judea eighteen centuries ago;
> that but for this belief the farmer would refuse to pay the tenth of the
> produce of his labours to maintain its numbness and idleness; that this
> class of persons if not maintained in idleness would have something else
> to do than to divert the attention of the people from obtaining a Reform
> in their oppressive government, & that consequently the government
> would be reformed, & that the people would receive a just price for their
> labours, a consummation incompatible with the luxurious idleness in
> which their rulers esteem it in their interest to live. (*Letters*, II, 143)

That is, the mania of inequality has been carefully inculcated by Christian
education. And when the conditioning is not enough, there is always
supplementary treachery: in 1817, the Habeas Corpus was suspended, and
agents provocateurs were planted to find people guilty of subversive activity, or,
failing finding them, framing them. The miserable injustice meted out that

year to the Pentridge leaders, Brandreth, Ludlam and Turner (Holmes, 384-6), hung (or, literally, was hanged) horribly in the air.

One considerable strength of *The Revolt of Islam* is that Shelley superimposes his supernatural labyrinth upon post-Revolutionary Europe, and the device, looking eerie and sounding exaggerated, yet ringing true, gives a poet's definition to the consequences of dogma – whatever species of political animal is guilty of it:

> It was not thirst, but madness! Many saw
> Their own lean image everywhere – it went
> A ghastlier self beside them, till the awe
> Of that dread sight to self-destruction sent
> Those shrieking victims …
> ……… and cried aloud, 'We tread
> On fire! the avenging Power his hell on earth has spread.' (X, xxii)

This epic poem shows that what has looked like the defeat of Liberty is by no means conclusive. Laon and Cythna are, finally, burnt at the stake, but the music suggests something other than death:

> And is this death? – The pyre has disappeared,
> The Pestilence, the Tyrant, and the throng;
> The flames grow silent – slowly there is heard
> The music of a breath-suspending song,
> Which, like the kiss of love when life is young,
> Steeps the faint eyes in darkness sweet and deep;
> With ever-changing notes it floats along,
> Till on my passive soul there seemed to creep
> A melody, like waves on wrinkled sands that leap. (XII, xvii)

The mysterious something-or-other present in music and poetry is the antidote to the "infectious gloom" the poet complained about in the Preface. The "kiss of love when life is young" cannot be quantified. Its power and beauty, however, can make things happen. A brother and sister can love and resolve to live together, and if the authorities will not let them live together, they can die together. The authorities can kill people, but they cannot kill what people have already thought and done, and continue to think and do, in the context of love's power and beauty. Like love, music cannot be quantified, and yet its power and beauty can make things happen. Music is present in the best poetry, which is, for Plato, "divine insanity" and for Shelley "harmonious madness."

The absence of an uplifting *je ne sais quoi* in a civilization's arts can suit tyrants and their drones down to the ground: "gloom and misanthropy ... the solace of a disappointment that unconsciously finds relief only in the wilful exaggeration of its own despair." (Preface, *The Revolt of Islam*) Peacock called it a "conspiracy against cheerfulness." It became the pessimism of the Victorian age, the nihilism of the nineteenth century, before turning into the ultra-nihilism of the twentieth – excellent for restraining insubordination without the need for state violence. An efficient government will be utterly dedicated to conducting detailed and ongoing management of the *zeitgeist*. Such a government retains and renews control over people by propagating emotive or palliative messages via entertainments to harmonise, and when necessary mobilise, mass opinion. If a government does this well, it can keep its use of batons, guns and tear gas to an election-friendly minimum. Hence the social realism, sex and sentimental trash sharing almost total domination over our commercial media. The idea of something important, magical or shamanic in the arts has come to seem at least as passé as manned barricades.

iv. 'The Mask of Anarchy' (1819)

Chancellor Eldon had ruled against Shelley in the matter of taking away his children by his first wife. By the time Shelley had married Mary and had two children with her, he was worried that they too would be taken away from him. This is why he was, as the first line of 'The Mask of Anarchy' reveals, "in Italy" at the time he heard the news of the Peterloo Massacre in September 1819: "The same day that your letter came, came the news of the Manchester work, & the torrent of indignation has not yet done boiling in my veins. I wait anxiously [to] hear how the Country will express its sense of this bloody murderous oppression of its destroyers." (*Letters*, II, 117) Shelley then quoted from his own work, *The Cenci* (1819): "Something must be done ... What yet I know not."

Two weeks later, he was sending 'The Mask of Anarchy' to Hunt, with a view to publishing it in *The Examiner*. Hunt did not publish it at the time. Had he done so, it is almost certain that both editor and poet would have faced prison sentences for sedition. The poem would not be published until ten years after Shelley's death, when it would be less dangerous to make public such an outburst.

The poem is influenced by Coleridge's 'Rime of the Ancient Mariner', but it is arguably a rougher reading, or listening, experience than the contemporary ballad-reading public would have been used to:

Next came Fraud, and he had on,
Like Eldon, an ermined gown;
His big tears, for he wept well,
Turned to mill-stones as they fell;

And the little children, who
Round his feet played to and fro,
Thinking every tear a gem,
Had their brains knocked out by them. (IV-V)

Admittedly, Shelley included personal antipathy, and this does account for the abrasive feel of many of the lines. But the overall achievement of the poem is in its capacity to convey the rightness of very strong feelings against a government demonstrably capable of murdering its own citizens, and standing over the corpse of Liberty. The poem's advice to the remaining citizens has the thrill of ambiguity:

Rise like lions after slumber,
In unvanquishable number;
Shake your chains to earth like dew
Which in sleep had fallen on you –
Ye are many, they are few. (XXXVIII)

This is exactly the kind of exhortation that will incense some people and incite others to salute the poet. On the one hand, it seems clear that Shelley is advocating revolutionary violence: there is no such thing as a vegetarian lion. On the other hand, the poet is walking "in the visions of Poesy" (I), and therefore not to be taken literally. The above lines could be said to exist somewhere between implosion and hallucination; they appear to have been uttered by the collective spirit of a people oppressed that has just found the strength to fight for its rights. The argument could go on indefinitely about how, literally and precisely, Shelley thought the fight should be conducted. Just as it never occurred to Blake to adhere to the facts when he included, say, the lion and the wolf in the same region of the planet (in 'To the Evening Star'), so Shelley naturally prioritised the refinement of a different mode of accuracy when he addressed the "Men of England, heirs of glory, / Heroes of unwritten story" (XXXVII). Any passive supporter of authority today, any somnambular consumer, could potentially – or so Shelley ardently hoped – be jarred into fuller consciousness by the following words:

What is Freedom? – Ye can tell
That which Slavery is too well,
For its very name has grown
To an echo of your own.

'Tis to work, and have such pay
As just keeps life from day to day
In your limbs, as in a cell,
For the tyrants' use to dwell,

So that ye are for them made
Loom, and plough, and sword, and spade –
With or without your own will bent
To their defence and nourishment.

'Tis to see your children weak
With their mothers pine and peak,
When the winter winds are bleak –
They are dying whilst I speak. (XXXIX-XLII)

Shelley pummels the reader with unupholstered political realities. The stranglehold that money asserts on human freedom is made vivid in the following three stanzas:

'Tis to let the Ghost of Gold
Take from toil a thousand-fold
More than e'er its substance could
In the tyrannies of old;

Paper coin – that forgery
Of the title deeds which ye
Hold to something of the worth
Of the inheritance of Earth.

'Tis to be a slave in soul,
And to hold no strong control
Over your own will but be
All that others make of ye. (XLIV-XLVI)

The card-carrying employee might feel in no real position to exercise rights whenever those in power diminish rights further and further. But Shelley has a special power with which to remind the reader that hypocrisy does not only exist in those in authority. He also reminds the reader that rights need to be fought (in *some* way) for, and won.

It may even seem unnecessary, *de trop*, to discuss what is repellent about gratuitously wasteful capitalism. Many people feel that it is wrong, and even fundamentally stupid, to work for bosses they despise, but they simply have to get on with it, as there are things to be paid for, and the money is not going to fall from the sky. One stark example of the sort of worker that gets on with things unquestioningly is the soldier, as Shelley would suggest in his *Philosophical View of Reform* (1820), "more degraded than a murderer", and "like the bloody knife which has stabbed and feels not ... beyond abhorrence and below contempt." (It is worth noting that Shelley wrote his *Philosophical View of Reform* in response to contemporary political economists, such as Thomas Malthus, who thought that poor people should solve their country's problems by not having children.) Most people will stifle their own sighs after a fairer life. To do so – one is encouraged, if one is detected struggling with the concept during one's school and university days – is to discover a degree of political maturity as a naturalised citizen of Babylon. Shelley's words carry a truth inconvenient for probationary Babylonians. The poet has the power to weaken any faith a worker might have in the ideology convenient to his employer. He can make workers ashamed of the conformist clichés that paper over the unholy pact with the enemy. He can resuscitate drowned hopes with the galvanic battery of his ballad's rhythm. The thumping music heightens and metabolises sensations that many workers (or those workers aware of them) would prefer to keep dormant in themselves, because of the certainty of their being left intellectually more scrupulous and therefore feeling even more defenceless. If you read Shelley 'too much', you become a 'danger' to yourself and to your co-workers, because Shelley's lines have the power to awaken in readers' minds the natural latent energies that promote in individuals the wish to band together and do something about injustice:

> And at length when ye complain
> With a murmur weak and vain,
> 'Tis to see the Tyrant's crew
> Ride over your wives and you –
> Blood is on the grass like dew! (XLVII)

One could almost catch an intimation of a justly incensed, rapidly coalescing mob, whose each individual member has just had a Shelley-induced Passover in his head, who has just cleaned out all the leaven, all the givens, and all the absolutes, shone a light on them, and put them through the third degree. It is just not true that the poet in question is a case of arrested development.

Of course, the strike-breakers can arrive and smash protesters' heads in with clubs as and when necessary, but Shelley has helped people shine a clear light on the science of media-manipulation, propaganda and control of the public mind – "Like a dream's dim imagery" (LIII) – long before Theodore Adorno or Noam Chomsky thought of such things, or were thought of themselves. There are lessons to be learned from the universal indifference that greets the extraordinary efforts of a figure like Shelley (be it remembered, born to an aristocratic heritage). And there are lessons to be learned from the (understandably) muted enthusiasm of publishers like Hunt and Ollier. If the *Address to the People on the Death of the Princess Charlotte* was published in 1817-18, there are no reviews of the pamphlet in any of the newspapers of the time. It was as late as 1843 when Thomas Rodd issued it as a stabbed octavo pamphlet of 16 pages. If it was published before 1843, it must have been limited and given exclusively to the parliamentarians Shelley most wanted (fondly) to influence – just as he had contrived to bring 'The Necessity of Atheism' to the attention of the bishops of heads of colleges at Oxford. 'The Mask of Anarchy' would not be published until 1832, and Shelley's 'Song to the Men of England' would not be published until 1839:

> Men of England, wherefore plough
> For the lords who lay ye low?
> Wherefore weave with toil and care
> The rich robes your tyrants wear?
>
> Wherefore feed, and clothe, and save,
> From the cradle to the grave,
> Those ungrateful drones who would
> Drain your sweat – nay, drink your blood?
>
> Wherefore, Bees of England, forge
> Many a weapon, chain, and scourge,
> That these stingless drones may spoil
> The forced produce of your toil?

Have ye leisure, comfort, calm,
Shelter, food, love's gentle balm?
Or what is it ye buy so dear
With your pain and with your fear?

The questions the poet asks of the men of England are limpid. The advice offered is enlivening in its simplicity:

The seed ye sow, another reaps;
The wealth ye find, another keeps;
The robes ye weave, another wears;
The arms ye forge, another bears.

Sow seed, – but let no tyrant reap;
Find wealth, – let no impostor heap;
Weave robes, – let not the idle wear;
Forge arms, – in your defence to bear … ('Song to the Men of England', 1819).

Radical action is needed. Better to be a rugged responsible workman reaping, keeping, wearing and bearing the products of your own labour, than a sleeping cog in a machine that benefits someone else. The concept of workers providing slavishly for the benefit of others did exercise the poet years earlier in *Queen Mab*:

what are they? –
The drones of the community; they feed
On the mechanic's labor; the starved hind
For them compels the stubborn glebe to yield
Its unshared harvests; and yon squalid form,
Leaner than fleshless misery, that wastes
A sunless life in the unwholesome mine,
Drags out in labor a protracted death
To glut their grandeur; many faint with toil
That few may know the cares and woe of sloth. (III, 108-17)

But by 1820, the more mature poet wishes to hear from Hunt "of any bookseller who would like to publish a little volume of *popular songs* wholly political, & destined to awaken & direct the imagination of the reformers." (*Letters*, II, 191) Shelley knew well enough that his hope would be considered a fond one. "I see you smile," he continued to Hunt, "but answer my question." (*Letters*, II, 191)

Having served time in Surrey Gaol (1813-14), and having paid a fine of £500 (and given a security of £750 for good conduct during five years), for libelling the Prince Regent, Hunt was probably very thoughtful about what he said and did. No wonder Shelley would have reason to complain: "Of the politics of the day you never speak" (*Letters*, II, 191).

However, there was still a fundamental misunderstanding between Shelley and most readers. His "*popular songs*" provided food for the radical thinking anterior to revolutionary action. And again here is the rub. How many readers are going to think along the same lines as Shelley when deciding what to do?

> We are all Greeks. Our laws, our literature, our religion, our arts, have their root in Greece. But for Greece, Rome, the instructor, the conqueror, or the metropolis of our ancestors, would have spread no illumination with her arms, and we might still have been savages and idolaters; or, what is worse, might have arrived at such a stagnant and miserable state of social institution as China and Japan possess.
>
> The human form and the human mind attained to a perfection in Greece, which has impressed its image on the faultless productions whose very fragments are the despair of modern art, and has propagated impulses which cannot cease, through a thousand channels of manifest or imperceptible operation, to ennoble and delight mankind until the extinction of the race. (Preface, *Hellas*)

Shelley's descriptions (of, say, the west wind, or a skylark) and his exhortations (to men to rise up against tyranny) can work very powerfully at a superficial level. Shelley's strength is also his weakness. In one sense, readers know where they stand. They know that Shelley has a passionate love of liberty and a passionate hatred of tyranny, and that the intense emotional significance which the French Revolution had for him was that it meant the liberation of that which he most loved from that which he most hated. However, many readers have found inspiration in Shelley without further investigation of the real point or lodestar from which the poet takes his bearings: ancient Greece.

v. *Epipsychidion* (1821)

In December 1820, Shelley met Emilia Viviani, the eldest daughter of Count Viviani, a nobleman of Pisa, and she became the inspiration for Shelley's greatest love poem (though Shelley's interest in Emilia herself would be outstripped by the mystical nature of the poem). Shelley said to Gisborne in October 1821: "The *Epipsychidion* is a mystery; as to real flesh and blood, you know that I do not deal in those articles ... The person whom [the poem] celebrates was a cloud instead of a Juno, and poor Ixion starts from the centaur that was the offspring of his own embrace." (*Letters*, II, 363) The object of Shelley's love changed "as clouds that veil the midnight moon" (to borrow from his poem, 'Mutability'), and the poet's belief in free love – and his opposition to the idea of marriage – is expressed most eloquently in the following lines:

> I never was attached to that great sect,
> Whose doctrine is that each one should select
> Out of the crowd a mistress or a friend,
> And all the rest, though fair and wise, commend
> To cold oblivion, though 'tis in the code
> Of modern morals, and the beaten road
> Which those poor slaves with weary footsteps tread
> Who travel to their home among the dead
> By the broad highway of the world, and so
> With one chained friend, perhaps a jealous foe,
> The dreariest and the longest journey go. (149-159)

The flames of the poet's passion are more empyrean than carnal, and this for many readers has made Shelley too remote to listen to when he is not addressing the 'Men of England' in plainer speech. The poem was published anonymously in 1821, and the strongest view of it, which appeared in a satirical piece in the little-known periodical, *The Gossip*, was on its incomprehensibility. "It [*Epipsychidion*] is an idealized history of my life and feelings," he told Gisborne, in June 1822: "I think one is always in love with something or other; the error, and I confess it is not easy for spirits cased in flesh and blood to avoid it, consists in seeking in a mortal image the likeness of what is perhaps eternal." (*Letters*, II, 434)

Shelley can only temporarily believe that in Emilia he has found at last the woman of his dreams, but the joy of such a discovery (however short-lived) is given a sort of permanence by the following lines:

> There was a Being whom my spirit oft
> Met on its visioned wanderings, far aloft,
> In the clear golden prime of my youth's dawn,
> Upon the fairy isles of sunny lawn,
> Amid the enchanted mountains, and the caves
> Of divine sleep, and on the air-like waves
> Of wonder-level dream, whose tremulous floor

Paved her light steps. On an imagined shore,
Under the gray beak of some promontory
She met me, robed in such exceeding glory
That I beheld her not. In solitudes
Her voice came to me through the whispering woods,
And from the fountains and the odors deep
Of flowers, which, like lips murmuring in their sleep
Of the sweet kisses which had lulled them there,
Breathed but of *her* to the enamoured air;
And from the breezes whether low or loud,
And from the rain of every passing cloud,
And from the singing of the summer birds,
And from all sounds, all silence …
Her spirit was the harmony of truth. (190-216)

Wordsworth had done something similar with his 'Lines written a few miles above Tintern Abbey' (1798), his poem of love to his sister Dorothy; Byron, too, had felt, somehow, in the natural world around him the presence of the love of his life, Augusta Leigh, from whom he had been physically separated:

In the Desert a fountain is springing,
In the wide waste there still is a tree,
And a bird in the solitude singing,
Which speaks to my spirit of *Thee*. ('Stanzas to Augusta', July 1816)

Shelley says in his 'Ode to a Skylark' that we look before and after and pine for what is not, and so his exploratory yearnings have left many readers looking at the discoveries with pleasure or in perplexity:

Warm fragrance seems to fall from her light dress,
And her loose hair; and from some heavy tress
The air of her own speed has disentwined,
Her sweetness seems to satiate the faint wind;
And in the soul a wild odor is felt,
Beyond the sense, like fiery dews that melt
Into the bosom of a frozen bud.
See where she stands! a mortal shape indued
With love and life and light and deity,
And motion which may change but cannot die;
An image of some bright Eternity;
A shadow of some golden dream … (105-16).

Just as Shelley had watched the skylark fly up into the deep sky and melt into the "pale purple", so the actual – and therefore temporary – object of his love refines itself into consistent invisibility:

> … a Splendor
> Leaving the third sphere pilotless; a tender
> Reflection of the eternal Moon of Love,
> Under whose motions life's dull billows move;
> A metaphor of Spring and Youth and Morning;
> A vision like incarnate April, warning,
> With smiles and tears, Frost the Anatomy
> Into his summer grave. (116-23)

Having made the natural world – "Of waves, flowers, clouds, woods, rocks" (511) and "quick bats in their twilight dance" (532) and "spotted deer" (533) – shine in the implosive aureole of his vision, the poet who fell upon the thorns of life and bled (in 'Ode to the West Wind') is now enduring the death throes of a martyr:

> One Heaven, one Hell, one immortality,
> And one annihilation. Woe is me!
> The winged words on which my soul would pierce
> Into the height of love's rare Universe,
> Are chains of lead around its flight of fire.
> I pant, I sink, I tremble, I expire! (586-91)

Even at the height of his powers, Shelley continues to provide his detractors with ammunition. "I expire!" might seem hammy to readers over-supplied with information about the poet's personality and encouraged to censure him. Hamlet's "Horatio, I am dead" and "O, I die, Horatio!" (V, 2) tend to be received less incredulously because critics know nothing of the author's actual life: for all they know, Shakespeare might have been every bit as delicate and *farouche* as Shelley the public schoolboy, and every bit as callous a user of women and as 'simplistic' a polemicist as Shelley the adult. But Shakespeare is completely hidden behind his art. If he was bad to his wife, no evidence of it remains to inform our reading of Hamlet's treatment of Ophelia. If he had a silly voice, no remembrance of it interferes with the shudder that Hamlet's gazing into the late Yorick's skull brings on in the reader. In the fullness of time, Shakespeare's contribution to thought has been declared elemental and set free. In the meantime, Shelley's remains on remand until the arrival of an unbiased tribunal.

vi. *Adonais: An Elegy on the Death of John Keats* (1821)

"I have been engaged," Shelley told John and Maria Gisborne on 5 June 1821, "in composing a poem on the death of Keats, which will shortly be finished; and I anticipate the pleasure of reading it to you … It is a highly wrought *piece of art*, perhaps better in point of composition than any thing I have written." (*Letters*, II, 293-4) "You may announce a poem for publication," he told Ollier, "a poem entitled 'Adonais'. It is a lament on the death of poor Keats, with some interposed stabs on the assassins of his peace and of his fame" (*Letters*, II, 297). Shelley and Keats have long been linked by *Adonais*, the elegy in which Shelley effectively professed his co-victim-hood with Keats at the hands of the *Quarterly Review*:

> The savage criticism of [Keats'] *Endymion*, which appeared in the *Quarterly Review*, produced the most violent effect on his susceptible mind; the agitation thus originated ended in the rupture of a blood-vessel in the lungs; a rapid consumption ensued, and the succeeding acknowledgements from more candid critics of the true greatness of his powers were ineffectual to heal the wound thus wantonly afflicted.
>
> (Preface)

Byron had little time for the poetry of a former apothecary with pretensions, and he had almost as little time for talk of medical matters coming from his notably unworldly friend. When, in *Don Juan*, Byron raised the subject of "John Keats, who was killed off by one critique", he was poking private fun at Shelley as much as public fun at Keats:

> Poor fellow! His was an untoward fate;
> 'Tis strange the mind, that very fiery particle,
> Should let itself be snuffed out by an article. (*Don Juan*, XI, lx)

Shelley's Preface to *Adonais* is a warm act of advocacy of a publicly hated poet. Just as Shelley had written in homage to the beautiful, recently deceased 'Princess' "LIBERTY" when most people around him were mourning the actual death of the Princess Charlotte, so with the death of Keats he was continuing to think and write in a fierce spirit of independence. In a way, it seems even as if Shelley wantonly dismissed himself from the serious thoughts of men of the world when he used phrases such as "these wretched men know not what they do." (Preface) The self-sufficient, defiant approach is radically different from Southey's modus vivendi. As Poet Laureate, Southey produced the long and ridiculous poem, *A Vision of Judgment* (1821), on the subject of King George III's death, and his inevitable entry into heaven:

> O'er the adamantine gates an Angel stood on the summit.
> Ho! he exclaimed, King George of England cometh to judgement!
> Hear Heaven! Ye Angels hear! Souls of the good and the Wicked
> Whom it concerns, attend!

Southey was determined to use the classical hexameter form, which was not used much in England because it was so unsuited to the English language. Shelley's use of a comparably difficult form (the Spenserian stanza) is more successful because of the superior subject matter and the superior author. The candour of Shelley's admiration for Keats, and hatred of Keats' enemies (his own enemies too), flows in a powerful, sustained way. The impostures in which the erstwhile Jacobin, Southey, became embroiled made his contemporaries point at him in hilarious disbelief. For example, there is the spectacle of the prompt, loyal Laureate attempting to squeeze through the pearly gates with the royal family:

> But the weight of the body withheld me. I stoopt to the fountain,
> Eager to drink thereof, and to put away all that was earthly.
> Darkness came over me then at the chilling touch of the water,
> And my feet methought sunk, and I fell precipitate. Starting
> Then I awoke …

In *A Vision of Judgment*, Southey eulogises a monarch and a regime responsible for death and injustice in America, France and Ireland. In other words, in *A Vision of Judgment*, Southey is sycophantic. In *Adonais*, Shelley eulogises an abused and neglected genius. Again, the point of view can seem simplistic: the poet's genius puts him forever at odds with the aggression, complacency, hypocrisy, ignorance, and all the other ingredients of a world benighted enough to insist on having in it bad kings, bad laureates, and the *Quarterly Review*. Death can sometimes seem like the only option for a poet:

> He has outsoared the shadow of our night;
> Envy and calumny and hate and pain,
> And that unrest which men miscall delight,
> Can touch him not and torture not again;
> From the contagion of the world's slow stain
> He is secure … (XL).

But the assurance with which Shelley articulates the insidiousness of worldly affairs – amounting, as he puts it, to the "contagion" of a "slow stain" – is uplifting for any reader weary on the worldly treadmill of consuming and useless emotions.

As in *Alastor*, the author of *Adonais* prefers to live in mourning for something great that once was, rather than accept the lesser reality he has been left with:

> 'See, on the silken fringe of his faint eyes,
> Like dew upon a sleeping flower, there lies
> A tear some Dream has loosened from his brain.'
> Lost Angel of a ruined Paradise! (X)

The mysterious speaker in the above excerpt, fanning Keats with "her moonlight wings" (X), is a producer of beauty and truth all the more beautiful and true because they come without machination: "She knew not 'twas her own; as with no stain / She faded, like a cloud which had outwept its rain." (X) Does the beauty of the lines lie in the sounds and syllables (which are, reductively speaking, mechanical contrivances), or in the beautiful metaphor of the cloud weeping? With the unobtrusive yet emphatic arrangement of the words ("… outwept its rain …"), Shelley gives a flowing, dissolving definition to the unforced being of the cloud. This is a perfect example of Shelley's (and Keats', and Shakespeare's, and Spenser's) ability to melt and recast the recognisable statuary at the gateway dividing the dreaming and the waking mind. With a Cellini-like virtuosity, Shelley has formed a train of tableaux in honour of a great (though unpopular) contemporary poet, and in the (unpopular) intellectual context that the human mind is not all-knowing, and that there are spirits. Keats had appreciated "the haunted air, and gnomed mine" (*Lamia*, II, 236) and their difference from "the dull catalogue of common things" (*Lamia*, II, 232). The Nature that Keats is now made one with is not dead, and it is not alive in any mechanical, or passive, Newtonian sense:

> He is made one with Nature: there is heard
> His voice in all her music, from the moan
> Of thunder to the song of night's sweet bird;
> He is a presence to be felt and known
> In darkness and in light, from herb and stone,
> Spreading itself where'er that Power may move … (XLII).

For Shelley, the recently deceased Keats is a living element of an active universe. Shelley wants to help transmit the news, because Keats' character was not fierce (like Byron's) or compromising (like Southey's) enough to achieve much contemporary recognition. Shelley has enough of the crude and insistent passion required to oppose "the total neglect & obscurity in which the astonishing remnants of [Keats'] mind still lie" (*Letters*, II, 366), and to make *Adonais* the monument worthy of the poet's greatness. The result is unforgettable:

> He is a portion of that loveliness
> Which once he made more lovely; he doth bear
> His part, while the one Spirit's plastic stress
> Sweeps through the dull dense world … (XLIII).

> The splendours of the firmament of time
> May be eclipsed, but are extinguished not;
> Like stars to their appointed height they climb,
> And death is a low mist which cannot blot
> The brightness it may veil. When lofty thought
> Lifts a young heart above its mortal lair,
> And love and life contend in it for what
> Shall be its earthly doom, the dead live there
> And move like winds of light on dark and stormy air. (XLIV)

In the concluding stanza Shelley suggests that the light of Adonais' soul is now shining out from "the inmost veil of Heaven". The poem is a superbly sustained expression of the freedom which an imagination free of cant and at full tilt can realise.

Shelley, like any other human being, existed as a bunch of sense-organs gathered for convenience at the top of a spinal cord enlarged and elaborated into a brain. Society encourages possessors of these organs to make prisons of them for themselves. *Adonais* transcends the restrictive matter (of chemistry, of politics, and so on) with a miracle: the solemnity, nobility, peace, intellectuality, serenity, and dignity of the poet and his subject answers the world's stupidity, rebukes its vanity, and kindles in the reader's consciousness an awed recognition of the human mystery, and the triumph of human life. When he reminded Joseph Severn of his promise to send him a picture of Keats, Shelley was keen to gain possession of something he considered a "sacred relic." (*Letters*, II, 366). He wanted to be able to look, often, at the image of Keats in the knowledge that the poet's essence was something altogether other than the clay that once bore the face's imprint. *Adonais* bodies forth a character deeply and pre-eminently tragic, but exceptionally difficult to fix and bring down into the definite world, because it exists beyond the definite world in the realm of thought, silent and invisible. The spirit of Adonais with which Shelley leaves the reader is a sublime idea – an outward and visible sign of the sudden apparitions of the mysterious world within us.

vii. *The Triumph of Life* (1822)

Shelley's use of the Dantesque *terza rima* is well-known: in the 'Ode to the West Wind' (1819), the poet used the form to convey the onward rush of autumn leaves, and political and spiritual hopes. In his last poem, *The Triumph of Life*, Shelley sets a scene of strange beauty that proves a perfect environment in which to experience a vision:

> Swift as a spirit hastening to his task
> Of glory and of good, the Sun sprang forth
> Rejoicing in his splendor, and the mask
>
> Of darkness fell from the awakened Earth;
> The smokeless altars of the mountain snows
> Flamed above crimson clouds, and at the birth
>
> Of light the Ocean's orison arose,
> To which the birds tempered their matin lay.
> All flowers in field or forest, which unclose
>
> Their trembling eyelids to the kiss of day,
> Swinging their censers in the element,
> With orient incense lit by the new ray
>
> Burned slow and inconsumably, and sent
> Their odorous sighs up to the smiling air ... (1-14).

Within the larger unity of nature, each hub of life unfolds its own unity of form in perfect, minute precision. The fragrance of the flowers and the light toward which the flowers turn are, in a reductive sense, merely among the many parts of the blind mechanism that most people take the world to be. For the conventionally educated mind, the atoms making up the external scene, supposedly no different from the atoms making up the observer (or participant), are inert, and driven hither and thither by external forces. Not for Shelley. On receiving "the kiss of day", the flowers swing their "censers". The rite of the morning is *observed* – by the Sun, the Ocean, the birds, and even the "smiling" air. The second and third stanzas quoted above fill the reader's beholding like a rose window in a cathedral. The one permanent reality, the underlying principle, is shining through the details of the world's phenomena:

> Before me fled
> The night; behind me rose the day; the deep
> Was at my feet, and Heaven above my head; –
> When a strange trance over my fancy grew
> Which was not slumber …

Poetic vision is inevitable:

> … for the shade it spread
> Was so transparent that the scene came through,
> As clear as when a veil of light is drawn
> O'er evening hills … (26-33).

All the outward circumstances and actual reality have become necessary as the laws and conditions of the visible world into which the invisible world is translated. Nature, where everything is fleeting, and everything is connected to everything else, can become the screen for vision:

> The birds, the fountains and the oceans hold
> Sweet talk in music through the enamoured air.
> And then a vision on my brain was rolled. (38-40)

Giving expression to his sense of the beautiful has by now become Shelley's chief occupation and delight. Mary Shelley remembered the triumphant spirit of the poet at this time:

> In the wild but beautiful Bay of Spezzia the winds and waves became his playmates. His days were chiefly spent on the water … At night, when the unclouded moon shone on the calm sea, he often went alone in his little shallop to the rocky caves that bordered it, and sitting beneath their shelter wrote *The Triumph of Life*, the last of his productions. The beauty but strangeness of this lonely place, the refined pleasure which he felt in the companionship of a few selected friends, our entire sequestration from the rest of the world, all contributed to render this period of his life one of continual enjoyment. I am convinced that the two months we passed there were the happiest he had ever known …

Shelley's happiness can be explained: he knows that the materialists are wrong, and he knows how they are wrong. They discard love and imagination. They put their trust entirely in reason in order to deal with life's challenges:

> they who wore
> Mitres and helms and crowns, or wreaths of light,
> Signs of thought's empire over thought; their lore
>
> Taught them not this, to know themselves; their might
> Could not repress the mystery within,
> And, for the morn of truth they feigned, deep night
>
> Caught them ere evening. (209-15)

How different are these people from Shelley! Their thoughts are so fixed upon literal ends that they see nothing in between. Shelley wants to reintroduce passion to the bloodstream of British thought, but the characteristically British fear of contamination has delayed the transfusion.

Shelley's writer-contemporaries' pursuit of impassivity amounts at best to collective sterility, and at worst to a collective abuse of humanity. He is like a spectator at a sports contest who cheers unrestrainedly and in a partisan way but does not miss an instant of the match. Some of his contemporaries mistake for keen and dispassionate observation what is really just an inability to cheer. (Remember Peacock's, and Shelley's, awareness of the conspiracy against cheerfulness.) They record 'the' facts (often hypocritically). But what facts, and why record them, unless to support pro- or anti-revolutionary rhetoric?

Shelley has been thrown into soaring passions, mindful as he has been of the powerlessness and vagueness of his conviction of the wrongness of the society into which he was born. He has often cried out, in the bitterness of his contempt, both for the tyrant and himself, leaving, in the process, some of the most humane and radiant poetry ever written. In 'Ozymandias', the poet grants even the pompous expectations of absolute power a tint of empathy:

> Half sunk, a shattered visage lies, whose frown,
> And wrinkled lip, and sneer of cold command,
> Tell that its sculptor well those passions read
> Which yet survive, stamped on these lifeless things,
> The hand that mocked them and the heart that fed.
> And on the pedestal these words appear –
> "My name is Ozymandias, king of kings:
> Look on my works, ye Mighty, and despair!"
> Nothing beside remains. Round the decay
> Of that colossal wreck, boundless and bare
> The lone and level sands stretch far away. ('Ozymandias')

Tyrants come and go like the clouds above, and the greenery in and around, the ruins of Egyptian monuments, or Anglo-Norman castles. Rats are eaten during sieges of cities, but not when the sieges are over and *coq au vin* is back on the menus. Royalist and republican vocabulary fluctuates and goes through wide changes of meaning. The words on a pedestal dating from *circa* 2000 BC will now be in a context different to the one in which they were first inscribed. The threat of social revolution can seem larger or smaller than the threat of counter revolution, depending on where one happens to be situated on the arc of attitude running through the seven ages of short-lived man. Shelley's faith is in something greater than the confused, slippery, wily, panic-stricken life of the human animal. Shelley's persistent expression of his faith flashes afresh like the light of a coal, sensible of a commitment to burning despite having been isolated from the fire.

Bibliography

The Poetical Works of Shelley (ed. Newell F. Ford), 1974
Houghton Mifflin Company, Boston

The Letters of Percy Bysshe Shelley (ed. Frederick L. Jones, 2 volumes), 1964
Clarendon Press, Oxford

Butler, Marilyn *Romantics, Rebels & Reactionaries*, 1981
Oxford University Press

Burwick, Frederick 'The Revolt of Islam: Vegetarian Shelley and the Narrative
of Mental Pathology' (*The Wordsworth Circle*, vol. XL, numbers 2 and 3,
pp.87-93), 2009 New York

Buxton, John *Byron and Shelley*, 1968 Macmillan, London

Christiansen, Rupert *Romantic Affinities*, 1994 Vintage, London

Foot, Paul *Red Shelley*, 1980 Sidgwick and Jackson, London

Forman, H. Buxton *The Shelley Library: An Essay in Bibliography*, 1971
Haskell House

Hazlitt, William 'On Paradox and Commonplace', in *The Collected Works of
William Hazlitt*, vol. VI (ed. A.R. Waller), 1903 Dent, London

Holmes, Richard *Shelley: The Pursuit*, 1975 Harper Perennial

Hughes, A.M.D. *The Nascent Mind of Shelley*, 1947 Clarendon Press,
Oxford

Hunt, Leigh *Selected Writings* (ed. David Jesson Dibley), 1990
Carcanet, Manchester

Johnson, Paul *Intellectuals*, 1988 Phoenix, London

Mazzeo, Tilar J. *Plagiarism and Literary Property in the Romantic Period*,
2007 University of Pennsylvania Press, Philadelphia

Medwin, Thomas *The Life of Percy Bysshe Shelley* (ed. H.B. Forman, 1913), 1847 Oxford

Notopoulos, James A. 'Shelley and Thomas Taylor' (*PMLA* vol. 51, no. 2), 1936 New York

Peck, Walter Edwin *Shelley: His Life and Work* (2 volumes), 1927 Houghton Mifflin Company, Boston

Plotinus *Collected Writings* (translated by Thomas Taylor) 2000 Prometheus Trust, Somerset

Praz, Mario *The Romantic Agony*, 1960 Fontana Library

Raine, Kathleen *Defending Ancient Springs*, 1967 Oxford University Press

Raine, Kathleen *The Underlying Order*, 2008 Temenos Academy, London

Rogers, Neville *Shelley At Work*, 1967 Oxford University Press

Rossington, Michael '"The Destinies of the World": Shelley's reception and transmission of European news in 1820-21' (*Romanticism* vol. 13.3), 2007 Edinburgh University Press

Shelley, Mary *Frankenstein*, 1818 Penguin Classics

Shelley, Mary *Journal* (ed. Frederick L. Jones, 1947) University of Oklahoma Press

Spender, Stephen *Shelley*, 1960 Longman, Green & Co. Ltd., London

Thompson, Francis *Shelley*, 1923 Burns Oats & Washbourne, London

Tomalin, Claire *Shelley and his World*, 1992 Penguin

Webb, Timothy *Shelley: A Voice Not Understood*, 1977 Manchester University Press

Woodring, R.B. (ed.) *Shelley: Modern Judgements*, 1968 London

Wroe, Ann *Being Shelley: The Poet's Search for Himself*, 2007 Jonathan Cape, London

GREENWICH EXCHANGE BOOKS

STUDENT GUIDE LITERARY SERIES

The Greenwich Exchange Student Guide Literary Series is a collection of essays on major or contemporary serious writers in English and selected European languages. The series is for the student, the teacher and the 'common reader' and is an ideal resource for libraries. The *Times Educational Supplement* praised these books, saying, "The style of [this series] has a pressure of meaning behind it. Readers should learn from that ... If art is about selection, perception and taste, then this is it."

The series includes:
Antonin Artaud by Lee Jamieson (978-1-871551-98-3)
W.H. Auden by Stephen Wade (978-1-871551-36-5)
Jane Austen by Pat Levy (978-1-871551-89-1)
Honoré de Balzac by Wendy Mercer (978-1-871551-48-8)
Louis de Bernières by Rob Spence (978-1-906075-13-2)
William Blake by Peter Davies (978-1-871551-27-3)
The Brontës by Peter Davies (978-1-871551-24-2)
Robert Browning by John Lucas (978-1-871551-59-4)
Lord Byron by Andrew Keanie (978-1-871551-83-9)
Samuel Taylor Coleridge by Andrew Keanie (978-1-871551-64-8)
Joseph Conrad by Martin Seymour-Smith (978-1-871551-18-1)
William Cowper by Michael Thorn (978-1-871551-25-9)
Charles Dickens by Robert Giddings (987-1-871551-26-6)
Emily Dickinson by Marnie Pomeroy (978-1-871551-68-6)
John Donne by Sean Haldane (978-1-871551-23-5)
Elizabethan Love Poets by John Greening (978-1-906075-52-1)
Ford Madox Ford by Anthony Fowles (978-1-871551-63-1)
Sigmund Freud by Stephen Wilson (978-1-906075-30-9)
The Stagecraft of Brian Friel by David Grant (978-1-871551-74-7)
Robert Frost by Warren Hope (978-1-871551-70-9)
Patrick Hamilton by John Harding (978-1-871551-99-0)
Thomas Hardy by Sean Haldane (978-1-871551-33-4)
Seamus Heaney by Warren Hope (978-1-871551-37-2)
Joseph Heller by Anthony Fowles (978-1-871551-84-6)
George Herbert By Neil Curry & Natasha Curry (978-1-906075-40-8)

Gerard Manley Hopkins by Sean Sheehan (978-1-871551-77-8)
James Joyce by Michael Murphy (978-1-871551-73-0)
Philip Larkin by Warren Hope (978-1-871551-35-8)
Laughter in the Dark – The Plays of Joe Orton by Arthur Burke (978-1-871551-56-3)
George Orwell by Warren Hope (978-1-871551-42-6)
Sylvia Plath by Marnie Pomeroy (978-1-871551-88-4)
Poets of the First World War by John Greening (978-1-871551-79-2)
Alexander Pope by Neil Curry (978-1-906075-23-1)
Philip Roth by Paul McDonald (978-1-871551-72-3)
Shakespeare's *A Midsummer Night's Dream* by Matt Simpson (978-1-871551-90-7)
Shakespeare's *As You Like It* by Matt Simpson (978-1-906075-46-0)
Shakespeare's *Hamlet* by Peter Davies (978-1-906075-12-5)
Shakespeare's *Julius Caesar* by Matt Simpson (978-1-906075-37-8)
Shakespeare's *King Lear* by Peter Davies (978-1-871551-95-2)
Shakespeare's *Macbeth* by Matt Simpson (978-1-871551-69-3)
Shakespeare's *The Merchant of Venice* by Alan Ablewhite (978-1-871551-96-9)
Shakespeare's *Much Ado About Nothing* by Matt Simpson (978-1-906075-01-9)
Shakespeare's Non-Dramatic Poetry by Martin Seymour-Smith (978-1-871551-22-8)
Shakespeare's *Othello* by Matt Simpson (978-1-871551-71-6)
Shakespeare's *Romeo and Juliet* by Matt Simpson (978-1-906075-17-0)
Shakespeare's Second Tetralogy: *Richard II–Henry V*
  by John Lucas (978-1-871551-97-6)
Shakespeare's Sonnets by Martin Seymour-Smith (978-1-871551-38-9)
Shakespeare's *The Tempest* by Matt Simpson (978-1-871551-75-4)
Shakespeare's *Twelfth Night* by Matt Simpson (978-1-871551-86-0)
Shakespeare's *The Winter's Tale* by John Lucas (978-1-871551-80-8)
Tobias Smollett by Robert Giddings (978-1-871551-21-1)
Alfred, Lord Tennyson by Michael Thorn (978-1-871551-20-4)
Dylan Thomas by Peter Davies (978-1-871551-78-5)
William Wordsworth by Andrew Keanie (978-1-871551-57-0)
W.B. Yeats by John Greening (978-1-871551-34-1)

FOCUS Series (ISBN prefix 978-1-906075 applies to all the following titles)
James Baldwin: *Go Tell It on the Mountain* by Neil Root (44-6)
William Blake: *Songs of Innocence and Experience* by Matt Simpson (26-2)
Emily Brontë: *Wuthering Heights* by Matt Simpson (10-1)
Angela Carter: *The Bloody Chamber and Other Stories* by Angela Topping (25-5)
Truman Capote: *Breakfast at Tiffany's* by Neil Root (53-8)
George Eliot: *Middlemarch* by John Axon (06-4)
T.S. Eliot: *The Waste Land* by Matt Simpson (09-5)
F. Scott Fitzgerald: *The Great Gatsby* by Peter Davies (29-3)

Michael Frayn: *Spies* by Angela Topping (08-8)
Thomas Hardy: *Poems of 1912–13* by John Greening (04-0)
Thomas Hardy: *Tess of the D'Urbervilles* by Philip McCarthy (45-3)
The Poetry of Tony Harrison by Sean Sheehan (15-6)
The Poetry of Ted Hughes by John Greening (05-7)
Aldous Huxley: *Brave New World* by Neil Root (41-5)
James Joyce: *A Portrait of the Artist as a Young Man* by Matt Simpson (07-1)
John Keats: *Isabella; or, the Pot of Basil, The Eve of St Agnes,*
   Lamia and *La Belle Dame sans Merci* by Andrew Keanie (27-9)
Harold Pinter by Lee Jamieson (16-3)
Jean Rhys: *Wide Sargasso Sea* by Anthony Fowles (34-7)
The Poetry of Jonathan Swift by Stephen Van-Hagen (57-6)
Edward Thomas by John Greening (28-6)
Wordsworth and Coleridge: *Lyrical Ballads* (**1798**) by Andrew Keanie (20-0)

Other subjects covered by Greenwich Exchange books
Biography
Education
Philosophy